Uncommon Ground

Uncommon Ground

A look at the distinctive beliefs of Seventh-day Adventists.

Morris L. Venden

Pacific Press Publishing Association
Boise, Idaho
Montemorelos, Nuevo Leon, Mexico
Oshawa, Ontario, Canada

Library of Congress Cataloging in Publication Data

Venden, Morris L.
  Uncommon ground.

  1. Seventh-Day Adventists—Doctrines. I. Title.
BX6154.V438   1984   230'.673   84-7690

ISBN 0-8163-0563-3

84 85 86 87 88 89 • 6 5 4 3 2 1

Introduction

Seventh-day Adventists hold many beliefs in common with the rest of the evangelical Christian world. Among these are their belief in the inspiration of the Bible, the Trinity, creation, the divinity of Jesus Christ, the sinful nature of mankind, and our need of a Saviour. We believe in heaven, and that the redeemed will live there eternally without sorrow and sin. We believe in the soon-coming of Jesus. We believe in salvation by faith in Jesus Christ alone. We believe that the devil is a real being, and we believe in the spiritual unity and mission of the church.

But there are some doctrinal pillars of the Adventist faith that are *not* common to the rest of the evangelical world. The purpose of this volume is to take a closer look at this uncommon ground, the beliefs that are more or less unique to Seventh-day Adventists.

We will examine first the messages of the three angels of Revelation 14, then the pre-advent judgment, the law of God, the faith of Jesus, the Sabbath, and the condition of mankind in death. An understanding of Revelation 14 provides a base for all the distinct pillars of our faith, for each is taught in that one chapter. But we will look at their basis in the rest of Scripture as well.

If you have ever wondered what it is that makes Seventh-day Adventists unique (it is something far deeper than going to church on Saturday and not eating pork!), we invite you to continue reading as we look at our *Uncommon Ground*.

Contents

Those Three Angels

Several years ago I was pastoring a church in Oregon. Someone said, "You should go and see the town barber. He likes to talk about the two untouchables, politics and religion." So I decided to go there for a haircut, and sure enough, in just a few minutes he was into the two untouchables.

He said, "What do you do?"

I said, "I'm a preacher."

"For what church?"

I replied, "Seventh-day Adventist."

He said, "Why are you a Seventh-day Adventist?"

I gave him a list of what I thought were good reasons, and when I had finished he said, "What church did your parents belong to?"

"Seventh-day Adventist."

He said, "Uh huh."

Then he continued questioning me. "Why are you a preacher?"

Now I thought I'd have a chance to redeem myself, so I gave him some good, solid reasons for being a preacher. When I had finished he asked, "What did your father do?"

I said, "He was a preacher." Right there I knew that it would have been far better for me if my father had been an atheist and a drunkard!

What this barber did not realize is that a person can follow in the footsteps of his parents only for so long. A time inevitably comes when he must study and learn and choose for himself. God has no grandsons. Whether you are fresh out of the woods, so to speak, coming from a completely nonreligious background; or whether you are a second-, third-, fourth-generation church member, I invite you to join in this study of the scriptural basis for the distinctive doctrines of the Seventh-day Adventist Church.

We'd like to have everyone understand why Seventh-day Adventists are different. It's not just for the sake of being different! We believe in the distinct points of our faith because we believe they are based in the Bible, and what's more, that the whole world needs to hear about them. So it is a real privilege to share these beliefs with those around us.

It is interesting to note that all of the six primary beliefs we are going to examine in this volume are found in one chapter in the Bible. They are taught all through the Scriptures, but they also show up in a single chapter in Revelation. Here in Revelation 14, through the symbol of three flying angels, are given three messages that are to go to the world before Jesus comes again. As you know, the return of Jesus is one of the major beliefs of Christian people everywhere today. These three messages are important in light of Jesus' return.

The first of these messages begins in Revelation 14:6: "I saw another angel fly in the midst of heaven, having the everlasting gospel to preach unto them that dwell on the earth, and to every nation, and kindred, and tongue and people." Why is an angel used to picture how the message will go? Have you ever wondered why the world went along for thousands of years with no particular increase in knowledge and scientific invention? To me this has always been a fascinating study. People rubbed sticks together or borrowed glowing coals from their neighbors for centuries to get a fire going. The Lucifer match didn't show up until a comparatively short time ago.

My Grandpa Nels, who came over from Norway, was frightened by the first automobile he saw, and so was his team of horses. My father was a boy, riding with him the day it happened. If my grandfather could come from the grave today, he'd think something drastic had happened! Why did the world continue in the same way for so many years? Was it because people were not smart? Not so. We're told that the average man on the streets of Athens in the days of Christ had the IQ of a university professor today. Greek philosophers are still known for their deep thinking. There must be some other reason.

Voltaire poked fun at Isaac Newton for predicting, on the basis of the Bible, that the day would come when man would travel at the breakneck speed of 60 m.p.h. Voltaire said it would be physically impossible. If Voltaire could come out of his grave today, still riding his old gray mare, he'd be a long way behind! Just a few years ago, a young man by the name of James Watt sat gazing at a teakettle boiling over a fire. He noticed the lid bobbing up and down, and something said to him, "There's power there. Get busy." He invented the steam engine. Robert Stephenson improved it, and it wasn't long until a steam train was traveling down a railroad track. The modern age of scientific invention had begun and has been going ever since. You know the story.

Why did the Bible predict that at the end of time men would run to and fro and knowledge would be increased? See Daniel 12:4. Because God wanted to provide all the means necessary for the last warning message to go out to the world with the speed of angels. When the prophets saw the end of time, and the gospel going to all the world, they didn't see a prairie schooner stuck in the sands of Nevada, or an old-fashioned sailing ship waiting for a wind to blow. They saw angels flying in the midst of heaven.

John saw this first angel flying with the everlasting gospel. There you have the giant pillar of the Christian faith— the everlasting gospel. The word *gospel* means good news. This everlasting good news is to go to every nation and kindred and tongue and people. It must be a universal and timeless message, so let's look for it.

Continuing with verse 7, we notice this angel "saying with a loud voice, Fear God, and give glory to him; for the hour of his judgment is come: and worship him that made heaven, and earth, and the sea, and the fountains of waters."

Let's back up and take the verse a phrase at a time. First, the angel gives his message "with a loud voice." A speaker who was reading this verse to his audience asked, "What kind of a voice would that be?"

A deaf man sitting near the front with his hearing aid turned up shouted, "A voice that could be heard!" He was right! This message is given so no one misses it.

The message begins, "Fear God." What does that mean? One thing we know it *doesn't* mean is to be afraid of God. Jesus made that clear. He gave us the picture of a God of love, tenderly guarding and guiding His children and working to draw all unto Himself. In the Bible, fearing God means to hold Him in awe, to respect Him, to reverence Him. But not to be afraid of Him.

I used to experience this in relationship with my father. I still do. I respect my father. There were times when I was afraid of him, when I had done something, or hadn't done something, contrary to what he was expecting. But it was by my own doing that I was afraid of him! So let's not think in terms of a God to be afraid of, for God is very patient with us.

There was a time when I had a real hang-up about the

hymn "Before Jehovah's Awful Throne." I used to avoid it, until a music major at college said to me, "You've missed the point. It is 'Before Jehovah's Awe-ful Throne.'" After that I began singing it again, and I have enjoyed it ever since! I am not afraid of God, but I hold Him in awe, because He is my Creator and I am created. One who is created should hold his Maker in awe. It's a principle of Scripture.

Let's go on: "Fear God, and *give glory to Him.*" There is a key phrase, a thread that goes through the messages of these three angels. We are reminded of justification, which has been defined as "the work of God in laying the glory of man in the dust, and doing for man that which it is not in his power to do for himself."—*Testimonies to Ministers,* p. 456. The phrase "give glory to Him" speaks of justification, of the gospel of God's forgiving grace. There is no glory for man in the work of the gospel.

But we are born glory hounds, aren't we? In one way or another we insist on our own glory. That's what so much of the entertainment world is all about. In the ebb and flow of men and nations, the glory of man almost invariably rises to the top. The reason for this is that we are born sinful by nature; we are born separated from God. Self-centeredness is the first symptom of that condition. We are all hopelessly self-centered apart from Christ, and would have remained so forever except for the cross. Although our own glory may go pretty high apart from Him, no one's glory goes high in the presence of Jesus. "At the name of Jesus every knee should bow" and "every tongue should confess that Jesus Christ is Lord, to the glory of God the Father." Philippians 2:10, 11.

The religious people in Christ's day were victims of self-glory, just as so many of the rest of the human race have been in every age. They blew trumpets in front of them, and their leaders prayed long prayers on street corners. They seemed oblivious to the fact that the Shekinah had left a long time ago, the glory had departed. The presence of God was no longer evident in their temple. Jesus warned them against seeking glory for themselves.

The apostle Paul said much the same in 1 Corinthians 5:6: "Your glorying is not good." And, again, in Galatians 6:14: "God forbid that I should glory, save in the cross of our Lord Jesus Christ." When he underscored his great statements on salvation through faith in Jesus Christ, he asked, "Where is boasting?" Romans 3:27. It is excluded, he said, in the light of the gospel. One thing is for sure, whether or not a person gets his name in lights here on earth or hits the headlines with his exploits—when we reach heaven, no one there will sing his own glory or give credit to himself for having been saved from his guilt or freed from his sins.

This is one of the two major threads woven through all the three angels' messages—a warning against self-worship, and an invitation to worship and trust God.

The next phrase: "Fear God, and give glory to him; *for the hour of his judgment is come.*" Here is suggested the unique pillar of the Seventh-day Adventist faith. We have believed for years in the pre-advent judgment, sometimes called the investigative judgment. We'll be going into more detail on this later, but here it is—mentioned in the first message of the three angels.

"And worship him that made heaven, and earth, and the sea, and the fountains of waters." We are invited to worship God instead of ourselves, *because He is the Creator.* It is a common denominator to all heathen religions that they have specialized in worshiping the created in place of the Creator. People worship the sun, which was created. Others worship idols or images which they have created. But do you have to worship the sun or bow down to an idol in order to be a victim of the principle of sun worship? No. You can worship your car or your house or your bank account or your good looks or your tremendous IQ. So the invitation to worship God comes to us today as well.

And the invitation to worship Him, because He is the Creator, comes in fourth-commandment language. Have you read Exodus 20:11 lately? "In six days the Lord made heaven and earth, the sea, and all that in them is." Here we find reference to another of the pillars of the Seventh-day Adventist faith—the day set aside in honor of the Creator of all the universe.

If we don't worship the Creator and give glory to Him, our only other option is to worship the *created,* because mankind is hopelessly religious and will inevitably worship something. And usually, when we worship the created, we end up in some way worshiping ourselves. People who have a poor image of themselves often end up worshiping other people. But we worship either God or man. It's just that simple. And the glory of man, whether it is our own glory or the glory of some other person, is temporary and quickly disappears. I still like the words of Charles T. Everson: "We live in a time when centuries are compressed into a few short years. Names of great men appear on the horizon, flicker for a moment, and then are lost forever in the sea of forgetfulness. But there is one name that grows brighter and more lasting with every passing year. It is the name of Jesus." No wonder we are invited to fear God and give glory to Him, and to worship Him who made heaven, earth, and sea.

Then we come to verse 8: "There followed another angel, saying, Babylon is fallen, is fallen, that great city, because she made all nations drink of the wine of the wrath of her fornication."

The word *Babylon* comes from *Babel.* The tower of Babel was a classic example of man's attempt to save himself, and you have a warning in these three angels' messages against trying to save yourself in any way. You remember Noah's

Flood, and after the Flood, the rainbow, which was a symbol or token of God's promise never again to destroy the earth by a flood. But the people said, "We're not sure God is big enough to keep His promise. We'd better help Him out." So they began to build a tower from earth to heaven.

This attempt to save oneself shows up repeatedly in Scripture, in the history of Bible characters.

God said to Moses, "I want you to lead Israel out of Egypt."

Moses said, "You've picked the right man. I'll get started immediately." He swung his sword and killed one Egyptian. He had to flee from the land of Egypt and spend the next forty years learning the lesson that Babylon is fallen. Doing-it-yourself has to fail. Trying to save yourself has to fail. It doesn't work; it never has, and it never will.

Nebuchadnezzar was king of Babylon. He used to walk on his veranda in the cool of the day and look out over a golden city in a golden age. He said, "Is not this great Babylon, that I have built?" Daniel 4:30. How easy it is to find ourselves in his shoes, taking credit for our own achievements!

When we lived in California, I tried to build a house. I had never built one before, but now I've built one twice! Everything had to be torn out and done over! But I found a strange reaction. When I'd finally manage to get a 2 x 4 in straight, I'd have to stand back and admire it for half an hour! "Look what I have done! Isn't this a great 2 x 4 that I got in straight?" It's so easy to be pleased with ourselves. Let's not criticize Nebuchadnezzar for saying, "Is not this great Babylon, that I have built?"

But Babylon is fallen. If I were to go back to visit my twice-built house in California and discover that it had come crashing down and was just a heap of kindling, it would pretty well destroy any lingering glory in my own heart for having built it, wouldn't it? Babylon, the city of Nebuchadnezzar, has been in ruins for centuries. It has fallen. The tower of Babel fell a long time ago. And in this message of the second angel, we are reminded of what happens to Babylon. It falls. The idea that you can save yourself fell a long time ago. The second angel invites us to recognize that Babylon and our own glory and worshiping ourselves are all fallen. We have inherent in this message a warning against trying to earn salvation by our own works and an invitation to the salvation that comes by faith alone in Jesus.

Let's go on to the third angel's message, beginning in verse 9 of Revelation 14: "The third angel followed them, saying with a loud voice, If any man worship the beast and his image, and receive his mark in his forehead, or in his hand, the same shall drink of the wine of the wrath of God, which is poured out without mixture into the cup of his indignation; and he shall be tormented with fire and brimstone in the presence of the holy angels, and in the presence of the Lamb: and the smoke of their torment ascendeth up for ever and ever: and they have no rest day nor night, who worship the beast and his image, and whosoever receiveth the mark of his name."

We'll look in more detail at this message of the third angel in the next chapter. But right now I'd like to dwell on the last part of the verse: "They have no rest day nor night, who worship the beast and his image, and whosoever receiveth the mark of his name."

When Jesus was here, He said, "Come unto me, all ye that labour and are heavy laden, and I will give you rest." Matthew 11:28. So the only reason for not having rest day or night would be from not coming to Jesus.

Sometimes we have looked only at the prophetic and historical interpretation of the verses, and they are important. We have studied the symbolism of the day of worship and have seen the connection between the Sabbath rest as explained in Hebrews 4 and how those who refuse it have no rest, day or night. But there is something far deeper here.

I'm going to take the position that anyone, church member or heathen, who does not know what it means to come to Jesus for rest day by day, and who does not give top priority to his time with God is on the road to receiving the mark of the beast and worshiping his image regardless of how well-informed he may be about prophecy and theology.

On the other hand, anyone who listens to the messages of the three angels and gives all glory to God, instead of glorifying himself and depending on his own attempts to save himself, is on the road to receiving the seal of God.

The lines are getting clearer every day. A polarization is taking place. The time is not far distant when all who are not totally committed to God will leave His service completely. The large middle group, with one foot in heaven and the other in hell, is fast disappearing. It is rapidly becoming a matter of all or nothing—and that's the greatest single sign that Jesus' coming is right upon us, for at His coming there will be only two groups. People will be either hot or cold, and the dividing time is almost past.

This is the basic message of all three angels—a warning against trying to save oneself, a warning against living life independent of God, a warning against counting anything else important except our personal oneness and fellowship with Jesus Christ. This is the message that will circle the world before the end.

What does it mean to worship the beast and his image? It means to worship self. You don't have to be a heathen and bow to gods of wood and stone, and you don't have to bow to some pontiff over in Europe to qualify. All you have to do is live your life independent of Jesus, and you're a worshiper of the beast and his image.

Then comes verse 12: "Here is the patience of the saints: here are they that keep the commandments of God, and the faith of Jesus." A saint is one who has been set apart for a holy use. That's the same definition as the one for sanctification. It reminds us of what God wants to do *in* us as well as of what He has done *for* us. In 1 Corinthians 1:2 we are told about those who are in Christ, saints, called to be saints, sanctified in Christ Jesus in every place, those that call upon the name of Jesus Christ. What does it mean to be in Christ? It means to be in relationship with Him, in fellowship with Him, in communion with Him. If you are in relationship with Christ today, you are one of the saints and you are experiencing the great truth of sanctification.

This verse reminds us of two more pillars of the faith; the law—the commandments of God—and the faith of Jesus. We'll be spending more time on both of these. Finally, in verse 13, the last pillar of the Advent faith shows up, the condition of mankind in death. Let's notice it quickly: "I heard a voice from heaven saying unto me, Write, Blessed are the dead which die in the Lord from henceforth: Yea, saith the Spirit, that they may rest from their labours; and their works do follow them."

So here we see in the three angels' messages all the pillars of the Seventh-day Adventist faith—the everlasting gospel, the pre-advent judgment, the Sabbath, the law of God, the faith of Jesus, and the condition of mankind in death. Through all of these messages, and through all of the pillars as well, are two threads. The one, a warning against self-worship, against trying to save oneself in any way; and the other, an invitation to worship God, to enter into the deeper life of fellowship and communion with Him.

As we accept anew the invitation of Jesus to come to Him for rest, and to keep coming to Him, we will know by experience the rest from trying to save ourselves. And as we understand the love of our Creator, we will fear Him and give glory to Him and worship Him, accepting each day the blessings of the everlasting gospel.

The Beast and His Image and Mark

We have noticed that the people at the tower of Babel didn't believe that God could keep His promise, and so they tried to help God out. Trying to save ourselves instead of trusting God to save us is a problem that didn't begin and end at the tower of Babel. And because the problem of Babel, or Babylon, is so ingrained in human nature, I'd like to take a deeper look at the issues involved.

So far we have noticed that two threads run through Revelation 14 and the messages of the three angels. One is a warning against self-worship; the other, an invitation to worship God. We can say it another way—a warning against salvation by works, and an invitation to experience salvation by faith in Jesus Christ alone. The person who is trying to save himself by his own works is worshiping himself; he becomes his own god. The messages of the three angels warn against trying to work our way to heaven and invite us to accept Christ's righteousness.

Some time ago I said to the speaker for the Voice of Prophecy radio broadcast, "I would like to talk to you about righteousness by faith."

He replied, "That's the only kind there is!" And that was the end of the conversation! What more can you say?

Of course, when we speak of righteousness by faith we must understand that faith is never an end in itself. Faith must always have an object. So it is righteousness by faith *in Christ*. Faith is not our Saviour; faith has never been our Saviour. Righteousness comes through faith in Christ our Saviour, and that's the only kind of righteousness there is. That is the theme of these three angels, and it must go to the world.

The righteousness of Christ has two aspects: The righteousness of Christ *for* us, because of His death and His life; and the righteousness of Christ *in* us, worked out through the presence of the Holy Spirit in our lives. Ephesians 3:17: "That Christ may dwell in your hearts by faith." Both the righteousness of Christ for us and the righteousness of Christ in us are the righteousness of Christ.

During the Protestant Reformation, Martin Luther championed the great truth of the righteousness of Christ *for* us, justification by faith. Later John Wesley taught the righteousness of Christ *in* us, sanctification by faith. Seventh-day Adventists are interested in both, and believe, according to Revelation, that there will be an emphasis on both of them together by the last church before Jesus comes again.

Whenever you talk of the righteousness of Christ, you are talking about Christ Himself. Righteousness is never separated from Christ, it is always a part of Him, it comes with Him. You never get righteousness by seeking it, you get it only by seeking Jesus. When Matthew 5 says, "Blessed are they which do hunger and thirst after righteousness," we could read, "Blessed are those who hunger and thirst after Jesus," because Jesus = righteousness. Righteousness never comes apart from Him.

Now let's read again the third angel's message, Revelation 14:9-11, and take a closer look at what it says. "The third angel followed them, saying with a loud voice, If any man worship the beast and his image, and receive his mark in his forehead, or in his hand, the same shall drink of the wine of the wrath of God, which is poured out without mixture into the cup of his indignation; and he shall be tormented with fire and brimstone in the presence of the holy angels, and in the presence of the Lamb: and the smoke of their torment ascendeth up for ever and ever: and they have no rest day nor night, who worship the beast and his image, and whosoever receiveth the mark of his name."

You'll have to admit this is a solemn warning message. Notice that you cannot receive any part of the beast without getting all of it. "If any man worship the beast *and* his image, *and* receive his mark in his forehead, or in his hand." If you become a victim of this beast power, whoever it is, you are going to be a victim of the image and the mark and all of it, sooner or later. This is a significant point to remember.

The subject has several natural subdivisions. There's the beast, there's a mark, there's an image to the beast. When you compare the scripture before and the scripture after, you find also a number and a name. Let's look at each of these.

Who is the beast power? It is referred to in the chapter just before, Revelation 13. The thirteenth chapter of Revelation is divided into two parts. The first half deals with a beast that has tremendous power over all the world. Why a beast? Well, perhaps because God looked down and saw men fighting one another like a bunch of wild beasts. At least there are similarities! Often, in prophecy, God depicts the nations of men by beasts.

The two books of Daniel and Revelation contain a history of the world's nations from 600 B.C. to the end of time. Daniel 2 has the table of contents; it lists the kingdoms which subsequent chapters will discuss. As any student of history knows, the first of these kingdoms, Babylon, was a world empire beginning around 600 B.C. Babylon was followed by Medo-Persia, Greece, and Rome. Rome was divided, represented by the iron and clay in the feet of the image of Daniel 2. Daniel 7 describes a period of persecution lasting 1260 years, down to 1798 A.D.

As you study Revelation, you discover that the beast of chapter 13 receives its authority, and even its headquarters, from another beast that went before it—which takes you back to Revelation 12.

Revelation 12 talks about a dragon which represents the pagan government of Rome that was ruling at the time of Christ's birth. Pagan Rome was followed by papal Rome, which ruled the world until 1798, harmonizing perfectly with Bible prophecy. Revelation 13 gives us a representation of papal Rome, which received its power and its seat and its authority from pagan Rome.

Papal Rome was a combination of religious and political power. We call it a "religio-political" power. It was not all civil or all political. As you know, it reigned in unquestioned supremacy for hundreds of years.

As you come to the last half of Revelation 13, you find another beast, an animal that looks like a lamb but speaks as a dragon. Many students of Bible prophecy believe the last half of Revelation 13 is talking about the United States of America. Certainly this lamblike beast has earmarks and symbols pointing to the United States. The last half of Revelation 13 reveals that the United States is going to set up an image, or a replica, to the beast that went before it.

So much for history and prophecy. One particularly significant thing about this beast—it gets bad marks in Scripture. "If any man worship the beast and his image, and receive his mark in his forehead, or in his hand, the same shall drink of the wine of the wrath of God." What's the problem?

We have noticed that the messages of these three angels warn against self-worship. If there's anything worse than one person worshiping himself, it would be two people worshiping themselves. If there's anything worse than two people worshiping themselves, it would be millions of people worshiping themselves. And if there's anything worse than that, it would be *organized* self-worship. If you study it carefully, this is why there is such a solemn warning against this power represented by the beast of Revelation 14. It is the greatest single organized system of self-worship that has ever been, and it comes under the guise of Christianity. This is why the beast receives such bad marks in Scripture.

However, please keep in mind that you don't have to be a part of a giant system of self-worship in order to worship yourself. You can do it sitting in any Christian church, if you are living your life apart from Jesus and His righteous-ness and depending upon your own righteousness, which Isaiah calls filthy rags. See Isaiah 64:6. Probably the most subtle form of worshiping the beast is to live our good lives apart from Christ. This has always been a serious problem for the Christian church—the idea that the primary issue in Christianity is just living a good life. We try so hard to live good lives that we have no time for Jesus.

I hate to admit how many years I wasted doing that very thing myself. I honestly thought that the way to be a Chris-tian was to try hard to live a good life. I got tired trying to be a Christian. Have you? I had exchanged the burden of sin for the burden of holiness. It was an equally heavy burden, and it wasn't holy!

When you are working up your own righteousness, the very thing these three angels warn against, you get tired. After I had been a minister for three years, it came to me as a surprise that the entire basis of the Christian life is in knowing Jesus as a personal Friend. That's where all the effort in the Christian life is to be directed. It's what makes you a Christian. If you have no time for that, if you are spending your time trying hard to be good enough to be saved, you are a victim of the beast and his image. That's why I get excited about these three angels. In their messages is the big dividing line between the real Christian and the one who only thinks he is. The vital issue is whether or not we come into personal, daily acceptance of the righteousness of Christ, instead of trying to develop our own.

Let's go on to the second symbol, the mark. You read about it here in the third angel's message and also in the previous chapter and the following chapter. Revelation 15:2 says, "I saw as it were a sea of glass mingled with fire: and them that had gotten the victory over the beast, and over his image, and over his mark, and over the number of his name, stand on the sea of glass, having the harps of God." These people on the sea of glass sing a song of victory and praise to God. What is their song about? Let's let the Bible interpret itself, for wherever the Bible gives a symbol, somewhere there is an explanation for it.

Evidently the mark of the beast is an indication or sign of the beast's authority. As we have read, you can receive it in your forehead or in your hand. The hand represents doing. The forehead represents thinking, or understanding. Some try to take the symbolism too far and suggest that there will be a literal mark, made with a branding iron. No, in the symbology of Revelation, this mark is received by either understanding or doing.

Now God has something that we receive in our foreheads too. He does not have something we receive in just our hands. You can read about it in Revelation 7, and we'll study it in a later chapter. For a long time Seventh-day Adventists have believed and taught that this has something to do with a day of worship, and this is right. However, there's something deeper than a day of worship involved, because the issues in the messages of the three angels are faith or works, doing it yourself or trusting God. Here is something that people often miss when they get into the question of a day of worship.

Let's look just briefly at the day-of-worship idea. Why

did God provide a day of worship in the beginning? As you know, the Sabbath goes clear back to creation. On the seventh day God rested from all His work that He had made, and He blessed that day and sanctified it, set it apart for a holy purpose. The Bible says that God has an interest in a tenth of our money and a seventh of our time. He has a real blessing for those who take this seriously.

The seventh day that God set aside in honor of creation was precisely that—in honor of creation. It was the birthday of the world. It was a weekly reminder that God is the Creator and that we are only creatures. According to Daniel 7:25 there would come a power that would think itself bigger than God and try to change the birthday of the world.

So there is more involved than just changing a day of worship. There is the issue of forgetting God as Creator. If we forget what the day of worship is all about, we've changed it ourselves, haven't we?

Now look at the name and number of the beast. These are found in Revelation 15:2, which we've already noticed, and also in the last three verses of Revelation 13. If we were to try to identify the beast in a historical and prophetic sense, we could do it from at least eight or ten different standpoints. Some people have taken off on one little facet and say that this beast can be identified by just the number 666. I was in a downtown religious bookstore not long ago and noticed books on eschatology and 666. The number of this beast is the number of a man, and the Douay version (Revelation 13:18) says the numeral letters of his name shall make up this number. Very interesting. Because for the title that has been given to the leading personage of the Roman power, the Latin title, is Vicarius Filii Dei, which some Protestants translate into numbers that add up to 666. But that is only one facet of the eight or ten different identifying marks of this power.

What is the deeper issue? What does Vicarius Filii Dei

mean? It means "Vicar of the Son of God," the one who acts in place of Christ. Go back with me to the Garden of Eden. Eve is walking through the garden and comes to a tree. There is a serpent in the tree, which we understand was a most beautiful creature at that time. The serpent looks through the leaves and says, "Hi, Eve."

Startled, Eve comes closer. The serpent says, "You're wondering how come I can talk, aren't you?"

Eve says, "As a matter of fact, the thought had crossed my mind."

The serpent says, "It is because I ate of the fruit of this tree. Now if I, a dumb creature, ate the fruit of this tree and became able to talk, what do you suppose would happen to you, who already know how to talk, if you were to eat the fruit of this tree? Why, you would become as God."

Eve listens—and we've been struggling with the results ever since.

As we have noticed earlier, three major deceptions took place at the tree. Two were doctrinal and one experiential. Doctrinal: (1) You don't have to obey God. He said you shouldn't eat, but go ahead and eat. You don't have to obey. (2) If you disobey God, the penalty won't be what He said; you won't really die. And the experiential: (3) Ye shall be as gods.

You know who was behind the words of the serpent. This was the first spiritualistic seance, and the snake was the medium. The devil was so successful with these tactics he's been using them ever since. He's going to close his whole program of sin on the same points that he started with.

I'd like to suggest that one of these days the ecumenists will put their heads together and say, "Why are we squabbling about all of our differences? Let's find out what we have in common." And as they compare notes, they will discover these three things: (1) You don't have to obey God. You don't have to keep all of His commandments.

There's one that is not that important. (2) You don't really die. And (3) inherent in the first two, you can be your own god.

The person who chooses to live a life apart from the faith relationship with Christ automatically becomes his own god. In this prophecy we find that a day of worship becomes a symbol of the one who is his own god, and another day of worship becomes a symbol of the one who has faith in God and trusts in Him and His righteousness. We'll leave that for now and go on to the final symbol, the image to the beast. *The Great Controversy* contains an interesting description of the image.

Before we read it, let's go back briefly to the biblical setting and remember that the beast of Revelation 13 is a combination of religious and political power. The image to the beast, to be set up, we believe, by the United States, will be a replica of the beast that preceded it, and so will be a religious and political power as well. But what is a religio-political power, and what is its purpose for existence? Here is where I'd like to use the words from *The Great Controversy,"* page 445:

"When the leading churches of the United States, uniting upon such points of doctrine as are held by them in common, shall influence the state to enforce their decrees and to sustain their institutions, then Protestant America will have formed an image of the Roman hierarchy, and the infliction of civil penalties upon dissenters will inevitably result." Notice that it is the churches that form the image to the beast by using the secular government to enforce a religious duty.

The government, of course, is human power. So the image to the beast is to enforce a religious duty by human power. Have you ever tried to enforce a religious duty by human power? I'd hate to admit how often and how long I have done that. Every January 1 I've tried to enforce some kind of duty by human power. There's no such thing as righteousness by resolution. There is only one kind of righteousness; it comes by faith in Jesus Christ. When you try to enforce a religious duty by your own human power, you form an image to the beast.

Let's stop focusing on the people out there and start looking at ourselves and squarely facing our problem. Trying to be a Christian by being good enough to be saved and enforcing all the religious duties we think necessary by our own human power—that's the image to the beast. It ends in self-worship, and there's nothing more clear in the messages of these three angels than the warning against self-worship and salvation by works.

Well, let's conclude with these hard lines in verses 10 and 11: "He shall be tormented with fire and brimstone in the presence of the holy angels, and in the presence of the Lamb: and the smoke of their torment ascendeth up for ever and ever: and they have no rest day nor night, who worship the beast and his image, and whosoever receiveth the mark of his name."

Seventh-day Adventists do not believe in eternally burning hellfire. Many others join us in that. We'll be examining this doctrine in a later chapter, but these lines sound a lot like eternal hellfire, don't they?

Remember that no doctrine should be based on a single text of Scripture. But one thing is clear here, there is a lake of fire at the end of this world's history. It is prepared for the devil and his angels.

There's something more! In Matthew 8:28 we read that Jesus crossed the lake of Galilee with His disciples, and, it says, they came to the other side, to the country of the Gergesenes, and there they were met by two men possessed by devils, "coming out of the tombs, exceeding fierce, so that no man might pass by that way. And, behold, they cried out, saying, What have we to do with thee, Jesus, thou Son of God? art thou come hither to torment us before the time?"

Devils were always uneasy in the presence of Jesus. They were in torment. When you read about the times when the devils met Jesus, all they could do was cry out in fear and plead for mercy. What does that tell you? That anyone who is ungodly will be uncomfortable and tormented in the presence of the godly. This has always been true. And anyone who worships the beast and his image and who is a victim of self-worship, will be in torment in the presence of Jesus and holy angels.

That's why it is an evidence of God's love that sinners are not allowed in heaven. They would be tormented there.

A friend of mine preached a sermon about a man who got into heaven by mistake. (He didn't mean to teach error, but to make a point. But someone came in late, and thought he was teaching heresy!) He set up a picture of a man who by some slip of the imagination got into heaven by mistake, and he couldn't stand it there. He was miserable. He began looking immediately for the first gate left open through which he might escape. It is an evidence of God's love that He doesn't allow sinners to experience the torment of heaven.

Then comes the phrase, "They have no rest day nor night, who worship the beast and his image, and whosoever receiveth the mark of his name." Notice the tense—they *have* no rest day nor night. It doesn't say they shall not have, or will not have, it says they *have* no rest. Present tense. The person who is trying to save himself by his own works, regardless of whether he is a heathen from the darkest corner of the earth, or a Christian who doesn't have time to spend in fellowship with Christ day by day—that person will have no rest day nor night. There is no rest for the one who is trying to save himself by his own efforts. The only way to escape the strong warning of this passage of

Scripture is to accept the friendly words of Jesus once more, "Come unto me, . . . and I will give you rest." Matthew 11:28.

Rest is a gift found only in coming to Jesus, and as we continue to come to Him day by day, we continue to receive the rest that He offers.

I invite you to spend as much time alone with Jesus each day as you spend watching television. Spend as much time in fellowship with Jesus as you spend eating your meals. Spend as much time talking to Jesus as you spend talking to an earthly friend. Is that going too far?

How often we settle for a text for the day with our hand on the doorknob. How often we say, "God, I'm so busy; you'll have to accept the will for the deed."

But Jesus invites us into His presence for prime time, deliberate time, planned time alone with Him. What an opportunity He gives us for rest! If I don't have time for God, I don't have time to live. His invitation is offered to each one of us again today, to escape from having no rest day nor night by finding rest in Him. In His presence we shall find rest for our souls.

The Hour of God's Judgment

How would you feel if the first thing you discovered when you got to heaven was that Billy Graham was missing and that Adoph Hitler was living next door? Impossible? Well, perhaps that is an extreme example, but we do know that there are going to be some big surprises in heaven. Some people we thought certain were going to be there will be missing, and others we thought sure would never make it will be present.

Someone handed me a little poem that says it well:

I dreamed Christ came the other night
And Heaven's gates swung wide.
With kindly grace, an angel
Ushered me inside.

And there to my astonishment
Stood folk I'd known on earth.
Some I'd judged and labeled
Unfit, of little worth.

Indignant words rose to my lips
But never were set free,
For many faces showed surprise—
They weren't expecting me!

The reason this sort of thing happens is that man looks on the outward appearance, but God looks on the heart.

There's a question I'd like to ask you. When you get to heaven, are you going to be happy there? Most people respond immediately, "Yes! Even if I'm the last one through the gates, I'll be happy."

But not so fast! Some of your loved ones and friends may be missing. The Bible says clearly, "Wide is the gate, and broad is the way, that leadeth to destruction, and many there be which go in thereat: because strait is the gate, and narrow is the way, which leadeth unto life, and few there be that find it." Matthew 7:13, 14. Few find it, not because it's so hard to find, but because few *want* it.

Are you sure you could be happy in heaven for eternity, if someone close to you were missing? Has God made provision, not only for getting us to heaven in the first place, but for assuring us that we will be happy there forever? These are heavy-duty issues that revolve around something that is known as the pre-advent judgment.

The pre-advent judgment, or investigative judgment, is the only unique teaching of Seventh-day Adventists. There are people in other denominations who believe as we do on the others of these six major pillars of our faith that we're studying in this volume. This is the only doctrine that is unique to us, the belief in a pre-advent judgment, a judgment-before-the-judgment.

An interesting text describes it. Revelation 14:6, 7: "I saw another angel fly in the midst of heaven, having *the everlasting gospel* to preach unto them that dwell on the earth, and to every nation, and kindred, and tongue, and people, saying with a loud voice, Fear God, and give glory to him; for *the hour of his judgment is come:* and worship him that made heaven, and earth, and the sea, and the fountains of waters." Italics supplied.

Some of us have felt in times past that the everlasting part of this message is to fear God, give glory to Him and worship Him. But it has also been everlasting good news that the hour of God's judgment was coming, and I'd like to show you why.

First, let's go back and see where Seventh-day Adventists came from. Seventh-day Adventists did not come into existence as such until the 1860s. Before that time there was a cross-section of people from many different churches who had gone through a great disappointment. There were Methodists and Baptists and Presbyterians and Catholics and others. They had listened to the 3000 preachers led by William Miller, who was a Baptist farmer turned preacher. These preachers had predicted that Jesus would come and the world would end on October 22, 1844. Their prediction was based upon a great Bible prophecy found in Daniel. It is the longest time prophecy in the Bible, lasting 2300 years.

But October 22, 1844 came and went. People waited from the early hours before dawn, all through the day, past midnight, and until dawn of the next day, but Jesus did not return. Scoffers mocked them, saying, "We thought you were going to leave us! Where are your ascension robes?" Many who had watched for Jesus' coming were embarrassed.

Some, as a result of this embarrassing disappointment, gave up the idea of Jesus' soon return. They gave up on God and faith and the Bible and the whole business of religion as well. But a nucleus said, "We will not give up. We cannot deny the presence of the Lord with us in our studies and in the meetings that we have attended by William Miller. There must be some mistake, and we will keep studying until we find it."

Remember, there was no such thing as a Seventh-day Adventist at that time. This nucleus came from various denominations. They continued to study, and they found the key to Daniel 7, 8 and 9, particularly Daniel 8:14.

These early advent believers had used the principle of interpretation of Bible prophecy that a day stands for a year. The verse in Daniel 8:14 says simply, "Unto two thousand and three hundred days [or years]; then shall the sanctuary be cleansed." They had assumed that the word *sanctuary* referred to this earth, that would be cleansed by fire at the coming of Jesus. But they took another look and did a word study on the word *sanctuary* in the Bible.

They were led back to the book of Leviticus and the Old Testament sanctuary service, with all its sacrifices and symbols, including a day of atonement or judgment that came every year. They were led forward to the book of Hebrews, when they saw Christ as our High Priest in the heavenly sanctuary. And to the book of Revelation, where in the passage we just noticed from chapter 14, they learned about the judgment of God.

As they studied, they came to this conclusion: That instead of coming to the earth in 1844, Jesus had a change of ministry, which marked the beginning of the pre-advent judgment. Notice again what the first angel in Revelation 14 says, "For the hour of his judgment *is come*." It doesn't say it will come, or it shall come, or it may come. It uses different language from what Paul used in his day when he talked with the rulers of the land and reasoned with them "of righteousness, temperance, and judgment *to come*." Acts 24:25. No, Revelation 14 says, "The hour of his judgment *is come*." Italics supplied. So these early advent believers became very much interested in these three angels of Revelation 14.

As they continued to study the comparison between the sanctuary that was on earth in Old Testament times and the sanctuary that is in heaven now, they came to the conclusion that the pre-advent judgment which takes place in heaven just before Jesus comes was what had started on October 22, 1844. As they studied still further, they found each of the six pillars of truth that show up in Revelation 14, and the time came when they organized the Seventh-day Adventist Church.

But for a long time there have been some people, even within the Seventh-day Adventist Church, who have had a limited concept of what this pre-advent judgment is all about. We have tended to think of the judgment primarily in terms of *us*. We think about God judging us and deciding our eternal destiny. Some have gotten the idea that since 1844 God has been poring over the books, trying to get through all the names before the end of the world. But there are bigger issues involved in the judgment than that. God doesn't need years and years to pore over the books. No, there's something more than being glad if your name is Williams instead of Adams! We need to understand more of the purpose of the pre-advent judgment, for us, for the entire universe, and even for God Himself.

Let's look first at the purpose of the judgment for us. Some have said, "We're not going to be present at the pre-advent judgment, so why is it important to us?" But wait a minute! God has made provision for people to stand on a sea that looks like glass and say, "Great and marvellous are thy works, Lord God Almighty; just and true are thy ways, thou King of saints." Revelation 15:3.

The people who sing this song, called the song of Moses and the Lamb, have experienced some big surprises. They may have looked for friends and loved ones and found them missing. They will have looked at the only thing mankind can look at, the outward appearance of those they have known. God wants them to understand the human heart and to see it as He sees it. The records of the investigative judgment will be open for all, and in this way we *will* be present at the pre-advent judgment. We will be able to see as God can see and understand the justice of His government as well as His great love. This will enable us to sing from our hearts, "Great and marvellous are thy works . . . ; just and true are thy ways." It is possible to sing that song and know that experience because His judgments are made manifest for us to understand.

I attended a large meeting where the question of the pre-advent judgment was being discussed. A man in the back of the room jumped up and said, "Who needs the judgment anyway?" It is a question that deserves to be answered. Who needs the judgment? As we have already noticed, we need the judgment in order to understand and accept the fairness of God's decisions.

Who else needs the judgment? Think of our judicial system as we know it. It is true that the accused on trial needs the judgment, ideally to get a fair decision as to whether he is innocent or guilty. But is the one on trial the only person who benefits?

In the first place, a case would never come to trial without a prosecutor. The prosecutor needs the judgment—in fact, demands it. Is there a prosecutor in the universe? Yes. You can read about him in Revelation 12, where he is called the accuser of God's people, the enemy, the dragon, the serpent called the Devil and Satan. The prosecutor needs the judgment.

There will come a time before this whole mess is over, when even the devil himself will bow and acknowledge the justice and fairness of God. Philippians 2:10, 11 speaks of it: "That at the name of Jesus every knee should bow . . . ; and that every tongue should confess that Jesus Christ is Lord, to the glory of God the Father."

All who watch a case in court need the assurance that justice is being dealt. If those who observe are unable to see justice in the decisions, their confidence in the judicial system and in the judge is undermined. Much of the corruption in our government today is reflected in the lack of confidence and outrage of those who witness the perversion of justice. If the people who are being governed do not have confidence in the justice of their rulers, there's going to be a problem.

Which leads us to the final One who needs the judgment—God Himself. Revelation 14 speaks of the judgment as "his judgment"—*God's* judgment. God is up for judgment, God is on trial, God is being accused before the universe as unfair, unjust, and unreasonable. The "accuser of the brethren" is also the accuser of God and has been hurling his accusations at the God of the universe for centuries. In order for God to be vindicated, in order for the entire universe, including us, to see that God is indeed a God of love and justice, in order to make the universe forever safe from sin and its results, the judgment must take place. So the investigative judgment is an extremely crucial truth.

Notice quickly four points concerning the investigative or pre-advent judgment.

1. There *is* a pre-advent judgment. It is announced in Revelation 14 by the first of the three angels.

2. According to Amos 3:7, God never does anything important without first revealing His secrets to His servants the prophets. So you could expect that if the pre-advent judgment is indeed a vital truth, it would be found in Bible prophecy. And indeed it is. You can read about it in Daniel 7:9, 10 and also verses 22, 26, and 27. The chapters of Daniel 7, 8, and 9 are a unit, speaking of the same period of time, and if you'd like to do some careful study on the pre-advent judgment in Bible prophecy, study these 3 chapters together.

3. Jesus Himself taught the pre-advent judgment. We'll take a longer look at His teaching in the next chapter. It's in Matthew 22, in a story about a man who went to a wedding with the wrong clothes on. It's a fascinating account that contains solid truth about the pre-advent judgment.

4. The pre-advent judgment is necessary in the justice of God. Notice Romans 3:26. Paul says it is God's purpose to

declare His righteousness, "That he might be just, and the justifier of him which believeth in Jesus."

As you study the purpose of the pre-advent judgment, three facts emerge. First, God is interested not only in justifying sinners, but in being just at the same time, as we noticed in Romans 3:26. The cross and the complete atonement justify God in forgiving anyone.

Second, the pre-advent judgment justifies God in forgiving the ones who get forgiven. As you know, not everyone is forgiven—only those who accept His forgiveness are forgiven. There is no such thing as salvation by grace alone—it is always salvation by grace *through faith*. And that demands that God's salvation be accepted by the sinner. God doesn't force His forgiveness on anybody. It must be accepted, and what's more, it must be accepted on a continuing basis. Matthew 24:12, 13 says, "Because iniquity shall abound, the love of many shall wax cold. But he that shall endure unto the end, the same shall be saved." The pre-advent judgment reveals those who have accepted and continue to accept His justifying grace.

Third, there is a post-advent judgment, or review, which justifies God in not forgiving the ones who are not forgiven. According to Paul, the saints are going to judge even angels. See 1 Corinthians 6:2, 3. Evidently he is speaking of the fallen angels who joined Lucifer in his rebellion. During the 1000 years spoken of in Revelation 20, the saints live and reign with Christ in a work of judgment. This is the post-advent judgment. During this time God will be justified for not forgiving those who are not forgiven.

Let's review those points quickly: First, the cross justifies God for forgiving anyone. Second, the pre-advent judgment justifies God for forgiving the ones who are forgiven. Third, the post-advent judgment conducted during the 1000 years justifies God for not forgiving the ones who are not forgiven.

The judgment is good news, for it reminds us that God treats His people as intelligent beings. God doesn't ask for our blind trust. One reason why we can trust Him now and forever is that that trust is based on understanding.

Another reason the judgment is good news is that God has committed all judgment unto His Son. John 5:22. Jesus is our Judge, and how could you find a friendlier Judge than Jesus? Jesus is our Defense Attorney and our Judge as well. He has never lost a case, so we have nothing to fear when our case comes up for judgment.

Finally, the pre-advent judgment is good news because it means that our custody is about over. Haven't we been in this world of sin, in slavery to sin and the devil long enough? When you have been sitting in prison, waiting for your case to come to court, and you find that the date for your trial has been set, it can be good news, for your custody is about over.

The good news of the judgment is that God still treats us as intelligent beings. The good news of the judgment is that Jesus is our Judge as well as our Attorney. The good news of the judgment is that our custody in this world of sin is just about over. What cause for rejoicing! The hour of God's judgment is come!

Wearing Work Clothes to a Wedding

Jesus loved to tell stories. That's probably why boys and girls loved to be around Him. He used stories for two reasons, (1) to reveal truth, and (2) to conceal truth. He wanted to reveal truth to those who would appreciate it, and He wanted to conceal truth from those who were working to destroy Him and His message. He said again and again, "If anyone has ears to hear, let him hear." For those who are seeking to learn the truth about God and salvation and heaven, Jesus' parables are among the most effective means of understanding truth.

One of Jesus' most interesting parables deals with the investigative, or pre-advent judgment, and in it we can see clearly the two aspects of the good news we've been watching for in each of these six major pillars of the Seventh-day Adventist faith. The parable is found in Matthew 22. Let's begin with the first verse.

"Jesus answered and spake unto them again by parables, and said, The kingdom of heaven is like unto a certain king, which made a marriage for his son, and set forth his servants to call them that were bidden to the wedding: and they would not come. Again, he sent forth other servants, saying, Tell them which are bidden, Behold, I have prepared my dinner: my oxen and my fatlings are killed, and all things are ready: come unto the marriage. But they made light of it, and went their ways, one to his farm, another to his merchandise: and the remnant took his servants, and entreated them spitefully, and slew them.

"But when the king heard thereof, he was wroth: and he sent forth his armies, and destroyed those murderers, and burned up their city. Then saith he to his servants, The wedding is ready, but they which were bidden were not worthy. Go ye therefore into the highways, and as many as ye shall find, bid to the marriage. So those servants went out into the highways, and gathered together all as many as they found, both bad and good: and the wedding was furnished with guests."

The plot thickens. "When the king came in to see the guests, he saw there a man which had not on a wedding garment: and he saith unto him, Friend, how camest thou in hither not having a wedding garment? And he was speechless. Then said the king to the servants, Bind him hand and foot, and take him away, and cast him into outer darkness; there shall be weeping and gnashing of teeth. For many are called, but few are chosen."

What was Jesus trying to say here? The first thing we need to notice is that Jesus was referring to a custom of the days in which He lived. When a rich person, particularly a king, put on a wedding for his son, not only was an invitation sent, but a wedding robe was sent as well.

This must have been an expensive custom! Most families today find it more than enough to provide special clothes for the wedding party without sending suits and dresses to everyone they invite. No wonder it would be an insult to the king for a guest to refuse the wedding garment provided, and to show up in his ordinary working clothes! But that is what happened here. The king found a guest who was not wearing the wedding garment.

Can you see him there, shifting from foot to foot in front of the king? The king is so kind. He treats him with dignity, which he really doesn't deserve. He says, "Friend, what happened?" Obviously there is something wrong! Most of us would probably have tossed him out on a moment's notice. But no. The king talks to him and calls him "Friend" and asks, "Didn't the mail arrive on time? Didn't you get my package? Do you have some explanation you'd like to make?"

But the man is speechless. Think about that for a minute. Why is he speechless? Obviously, because he has nothing to say. He has not shown up at the wedding minus the wedding garment because of any misunderstanding on his part or because of any lack on the part of the king. The wedding garment was offered to him, and he has refused to accept it. He is not a victim of circumstances or of an unfortunate background. He is speechless because he is without excuse.

And it is only after the king has made certain that this is the case that the man is shown to the exit.

The next thing we can notice about this parable is that Jesus, in His usual style, was hiding truth and revealing truth. He was giving a picture of the Jewish nation and how they had turned down the invitation to the wedding. It says the king was wroth and sent forth his armies, destroyed those murderers, and burned up their city. Jesus here made a prediction, in parable form, of the destruction of Jerusalem.

The king said to his servants, "The wedding is ready, but they which are bidden were not worthy." Right here we need to notice what it is that makes a person worthy. Have you ever heard one of those prayers that are clichés from beginning to end, so that you can predict what every next phrase will be? "'And then, Lord, at last when Thou comest in the clouds, grant that we, without the loss of one, may be worthy to have an abundant entrance into Thy kingdom." Does it sound familiar? What do you think of when you hear the word *worthy?* We often think, "Am I going to be good enough to make it?" We measure ourselves by ourselves and wonder whether we will be worthy. But please notice that the only reason the invitees were not worthy was that they had not accepted the invitation. The only thing that would have made them worthy was to have accepted the invitation. It's as simple as that.

So the servants went out into the highway and gathered all, as many as they found, both bad and good. There you have the gospel being taken to the Gentiles, which includes you and me down to this present moment.

Jesus said the servants gathered "both bad and good." How many good people are there? Romans 3:10 says, "There is none righteous, no, not one." So who are the good? There are bad people who know they are bad, and there are bad people who think they are good. But we're all bad. We are all born separated from God and are prone to sin by nature. The Bible is very clear on that point. But at least, if the bad and good are both invited, this assures each one of us that we are included in the invitation. The marriage supper of the Lamb is open to all. Here is the great truth of justification. Jesus at the cross gained the right to forgive anyone and offer him a place at the wedding.

Notice what Revelation 19 says about this marriage supper of the Lamb. Begin with verse 6: "I heard as it were the voice of a great multitude, and as the voice of many waters, and as the voice of mighty thunderings, saying, Alleluia: for the Lord God omnipotent reigneth. Let us be glad and rejoice, and give honour to him: for the marriage of the Lamb is come, and his wife hath made herself ready. And to her was granted that she should be arrayed in fine linen, clean and white: for the fine linen is the righteousness of saints." That's the King James Version. The more accurate New International Version says, "fine linen stands for righteous acts of the saints." This is what most of the new versions say, something relative to deeds, or acts, of the saints. It obviously refers to the righteousness of Christ worked out in the life, not just the righteousness of Christ for us. "He saith unto me, Write, Blessed are they which are called unto the marriage supper of the Lamb." Verse 9.

The next thing we see in this parable is that the marriage supper takes place pre-advent. It's in a pre-advent context both in Matthew 22 and Revelation 19. So as you follow through this story about the wedding, you are taken right into Jesus' teaching on the pre-advent judgment.

Let's take a closer look. All have been invited to the marriage supper, both bad and good. The king comes in to see the guests. The king comes in to *examine* the guests. Shall we go so far as to say the king comes in to *investigate* the guests? He sees a man who is not wearing a wedding garment.

What is the wedding garment? It is the righteous deeds, the righteous acts of the saints, suggesting Christ's righteousness in us, sanctification. Where do the saints get their righteousness? They are incapable of producing it. It is always "the Lord our righteousness." Jeremiah 23:6.

Revelation 3:5 talks about this too. "He that overcometh, the same shall be clothed in white raiment; and I will not blot out his name out of the book of life." There you have sanctuary and judgment language again. "But I will confess his name before my Father, and before his angels."

Some people say, "Wait a minute. You're taking away my assurance of salvation when you talk about overcoming and putting on a robe." I'd like to remind you that if overcoming were my work, there would be good reason for me to be nervous. In fact, there would be nothing but hopelessness. The truth is that overcoming is Jesus' work—a truth that has evaded many of us. The invitation is free to all, both bad and good. But if you are to be consistent with Scripture, you cannot deny that there is a robe and that the robe has to do with overcoming, with the righteousness of Christ *in* us.

When the man was asked about the robe, he was speechless. He had nothing to say. God never holds us accountable for what we do not understand. The man must have understood about the robe and turned it down. Only then was he dismissed from the marriage feast.

But if our hope of eternal life is based totally on what Jesus did at the cross, what does this overcoming have to do with it? It reminds me of the evangelist who said, "We do not get to heaven by keeping the law, but we can't get to heaven if we don't keep it. We don't get to heaven by putting on the robe, but we can't get to heaven without it." Is this diluting the gospel of God's free grace?

Perhaps a little illustration will help. When I was living in California, the college in town hired professors to teach there on the basis of their expertise, their training, their degree, their study. They invited them to come on that basis. But every professor who came to teach had to take a TB test, because it just so happened that the board and faculty didn't want any teacher going around campus coughing and sneezing tuberculosis germs on everyone else. The TB test had nothing to do with the basis on which someone was invited to teach, but passing the TB test was still a condition for teaching there.

The invitation that Jesus gives to everyone to come to the marriage supper of the Lamb is based totally on what Jesus has done, and what Jesus has done is enough. That is the basis for the invitation. But it just so happens that God doesn't want people coughing and sneezing sin germs all over His universe, so He has made putting on the robe a condition for entrance into heaven.

Well, you may say, regardless of how it is explained, it still comes out the same. There goes my assurance. There goes my certainty of salvation. I guess I'll have to change my theology to match my performance. I guess I don't want all the truth in this parable.

Suppose I came to you and said, "I have a brand-new Cadillac Seville that I want to give you, with the down payment absolutely free. Would you like a new Cadillac with no down payment?"

What would be one of your first questions? "How much are the monthly payments going to be?"

Well, the monthly payments are $1000 a month for the rest of your life! Are you interested? Why, you'd tell me to forget it!

Suppose the Lord Jesus comes to you today and says, "I have made provision at the cross to give you a free invitation to the marriage supper of the Lamb. But you have to wear a wedding garment in order to be admitted, and you have to make it yourself. The garment must be absolutely perfect, without one flaw. Without the wedding garment, you will be shut out of the wedding."

Let me ask you: Have you accepted the invitation to the wedding? Have you accepted God's justifying grace, made available because of the cross? Are you also wearing the wedding garment? That gets a little heavier, doesn't it? If the wedding garment seems impossible, there appears to be only one option, and that is to walk away from the invitation.

But there is one thing you may have missed. It is this: The wedding garment is just as free as the invitation. Did you understand that sentence? Let's repeat it: THE WEDDING GARMENT IS JUST AS FREE AS THE INVITATION. Don't miss that! The wedding garment is free. It's a gift.

What are we saying by that? We're saying that sanctification is just as much a gift as is justification. Obedience is just as much a gift as is forgiveness. Overcoming is just as much a gift as is pardon. It's not something you achieve; it's something you receive. I invite you to ask God to help you understand and experience this truth, because it's the only thing that can give us hope of having on the wedding garment when the king comes in to examine the guests. If it wasn't true that the robe is as free as the invitation, there wouldn't be a chance for any of us. We cannot produce one bit of righteousness, either *for* ourselves or *in* ourselves. It must all be of Christ. Do you believe that? Do you accept it?

The robe is as free as the invitation! I wish I could say it fifty different times in fifty different ways. The robe is as free as the invitation. The reason we have not overcome, the reason why we have to drag God's truth down to our level of performance, and the reason why we feel threatened by the judgment and perfection and all the rest of it is that we have not seen this point, that the robe is as free as the invitation.

I invite you to ask the Lord to show you how this can work out in your own personal life, as you seek fellowship with Him day by day. The invitation of grace is accepted by coming to Him in prayer and the study of His Word. The wedding garment is received in the same way. All that we can do to accept His free gift of both these aspects of His righteousness is to come into His presence—and the way we come into His presence is in our private time alone with Him. As we continue to come to Him, He makes Himself responsible for teaching us all the truth that He has for us to learn and experience in preparation for eternity with Him.

In the meantime, wouldn't you like to RSVP? The King invites you to the marriage supper of the Lamb. Which way will you reply?

"To the King of kings and Lord of lords: I have received Your invitation to be present at the marriage supper of Your Son, Jesus. I pray Thee, have me excused."

Or, "To the King of kings and Lord of lords: I have just received Your urgent invitation to be present at the marriage supper of Your only-begotten Son. I hasten to reply, By the grace of God, I'll be there. P.S. And thank You for the beautiful robe."

Law and Grace

Once while I was living in Los Angeles, I drove by some street construction. Without realizing it, because it was covered with dirt, I crossed over a double yellow line, which was against the law. A police officer saw me. He stopped me and gave me a ticket. I tried to explain, but he wouldn't listen. It was one of the times when I was not very happy with the law!

Well, I decided to go to court and explain my situation to the judge. Like any other court in Southern California, that court was full of people. I sat through the entire forenoon waiting for my name to come up. I didn't realize I was supposed to turn in my ticket at the window before I went into the courtroom. I assumed that I had to wait because my name was toward the end of the alphabet. Finally all the other cases had been tried, and the courtroom was emptied. I was the only one remaining.

The judge said, "You came to visit today?"

"No," I said. "I came to take care of my traffic citation."

"Did you turn your ticket in at the window?"

"No."

So he said, "Well, give it to me." I gave him my ticket and explained about the construction area and the lines covered with dirt. He thought it was a good explanation and dismissed my case.

49

Although I wasn't necessarily any happier with the law, I was certainly happy with that judge!

As we consider the pillar of faith which is known as the law of God, I make no apologies for talking about law. Some people say we should talk only about love, that talking about the law is legalistic. But *love* is an abstract word. I dare you to define what love is. We can tell how it works and what it does, but to define love is hard.

A friend of mine had a sister who was in love and planning to get married. He went to her one day and said, "Sis, you're in love?"

"Yes."

He said, "Will you do me a favor?"

"Yes."

"Will you tell me what love is? Give me a definition so I'll know what love is."

She said, "Sure. Love is, that thing, . . . uh, love is . . . uh, love is the way . . . er, uh, love is what happens when . . . I don't know."

The longer she tried for a definition, the further she got from it. Love is something like strawberry shortcake. You can experience it, but it is impossible to give an adequate definition for it.

Because of its lack of definition, love has often been misunderstood and cheapened. People have killed other people for "love" of their country. People have left families, husbands and wives and children for a new "love." Love needs boundaries. Love needs definition. The law of God is friendly because it describes what real love is all about. Without it we are like ships without a sail or rudder or compass. Your opinion is no better than mine, and mine is no better than yours as to what love is, without the law of God.

The early Adventist pioneers became very much aware of the law of God because of events that took place in their lives. You remember that 3,000 preachers joined William

Miller in preaching that Jesus was going to come in 1844. Jesus didn't come in 1844, and most of the followers of this great excitement gave up the faith and had nothing more to do with it. But some insisted that what they had experienced was real and continued to search and study to find what they had misunderstood. In the process, their attention was directed to the heavenly sanctuary. They saw a courtyard, a first apartment, and a second apartment. In that second apartment was the ark of the covenant. In this ark were the Ten Commandments.

As they focused on the law of God, they realized a deeper appreciation for the gospel and for the atonement. Some keen minds began to do a little reasoning, based upon human law and courts and governments. I suppose you are aware that most governments are based to some extent upon the Ten Commandments. Legislators and governors and lawmakers of all types have understood the validity of law and government and the validity of God's law.

Now here is a simple premise of any government, one I have mentioned to you before. A government is no stronger than its laws. No law is stronger than the penalty for breaking it. No penalty is stronger than its enforcement. It's a basic rule of all government. So if God's law is the foundation of His government, if God's law were to go down, God Himself would go down. But the Bible says that God is forever; therefore His law is forever and His government will not go down. It's just that simple.

Any government would go down, and any law would be of no effect if it could be transgressed without penalty. This is what the atonement and the cross are all about. God had a system in mind before the foundation of the world that included His being reconciled to the world *with* His Son at the cross, which would nail down forever the premise that God's law *cannot* be changed.

Laws have been changed in our country, even after people have died because of them. It doesn't make sense. The first parents who lost their son in the state of Oregon as a result of capital punishment had good reason to be upset when later that penalty was rescinded. Their son had died. If the law could be changed later, why couldn't it have been changed earlier? It's a good question, isn't it?

But God doesn't operate by the ebb and flow of popular demand. He says, "If the law is broken, the penalty will be paid, even if We have to pay it Ourselves." Jesus' death on the cross proved that God's law would never be changed. As the Advent pioneers who studied this subject began to realize how far-reaching and how sensible and how loving is the gospel of the atonement, they began to appreciate God's law in a new way.

Their understanding of God's law in its broader form gave our pioneers a new appreciation for the gospel. As you know, the Bible speaks of the law as our schoolmaster, or truant officer. See Galatians 3:24. The schoolmaster is the one who takes a child who is playing hooky back to school. The law is our schoolmaster in at least two ways. First, when we look at our past record, at our sins and failures, the law takes us to the foot of the cross for forgiveness, to accept again the fact that "if we confess our sins, he is faithful and just to forgive us our sins, and to cleanse us from all unrighteousness." 1 John 1:9.

The second way that the law is our schoolmaster is that when we look at the law and measure our present living against it, we realize our struggles as growing Christians are inadequate, and the law brings us to Christ for power. Therefore the law is one of the greatest evidences for helping us to realize our need of Jesus and His love and strength.

As you study the history of these pillars of faith, you discover that since 1844 two streams of thought have emerged—whether we can obey or whether we can't obey. Different positions are taken by what is called the remnant, and by what we might call the nominal Christian world. Now please, when I use the term *nominal Christian world* I am not talking about anyone who is not a part of the remnant. *Nominal Christian* means Christian in name only. Those who have been Christians in name only have been the ones who have taken the position that God's law is not important, that it cannot be kept, that it is impossible to obey, and that all we do, as Christians, is go to the cross and believe. That's the position of the nominal Christian world.

There is a group in Bible prophecy which is identified as the remnant and which could include people in every walk who still believe that God and His law are important, and who still believe that it is possible through the power of God to obey the commandments. Revelation 14:12 talks about this group who are alive just before Jesus comes again: "Here is the patience of the saints: here are they that keep the commandments of God, and the faith of Jesus."

There's something about this text that gives hope and comfort. The saints are going to be known for their patience, and usually we think of patience in terms of being patient with one another. Let's allow for the possibility that the saints are also going to be patient with themselves. They will not give up in discouragement when it seems that the progress in their lives is slow, because God knows what He is working with and has given assurance that the blade comes first, then the ear, and after that the full corn in the ear. So let's be as patient with ourselves as God is.

The second thing we notice about this group is that they keep the commandments of God, which some people today think needs explanation. They take off on the word *keep* and say, "This doesn't mean to obey. It means *keep* as in *keeping* sheep, for instance; to *watch over* the sheep. The sheep keeper protects and defends the sheep. *Keep* can't mean to *obey*, because it's impossible for anyone to obey all the commandments."

But if you do a word study on the word *keep* through the Scriptures, which I will spare you at the moment, you will discover that *keep* not only means to guard and watch over and defend, but to *translate into action*. Probably one of your best texts on that would be in Matthew 19, where the rich young ruler comes and says to Jesus, "Good Master, what good thing shall I do, that I may have eternal life?" Jesus says, "Keep the commandments." The young man replies, "I have done all that. 'All those things have I *kept* from my youth up.' " *Keep* has to do with behavior and action. Read the context. The dialog continues with Jesus trying to show the rich young ruler that he really needs to accept the law as a schoolmaster to bring him to the feet of Jesus for the power which he lacks.

So in Revelation 14:12 we have a group of people who keep the commandments of God. They don't just believe that the commandments are nice, but they keep them. And they have the faith of Jesus, which leads us to another significant observation. It isn't safe to talk about the law of God without talking about the faith of Jesus. We will study more into the faith of Jesus in the chapters on that topic. But the faith of Jesus was also one of the pillars of the faith of the Advent pioneers. The law of God and the faith of Jesus go together. There's no hope for obeying the law of God without the faith of Jesus. That's why we want to spend some time on that subject before we're finished with this volume.

The other text in Revelation that goes along with this one we have just studied is chapter 12, verse 17. The dragon, or the devil, is angry with the woman, or the church. He "went to make war with the remnant of her seed, which keep the commandments of God, and have the testimony of Jesus."

At the very end of this earth's history, obedience or disobedience is the question to be decided by the whole world. We live in an interesting time, when both without and within the church voices are debating this question of obedience versus disobedience.

But wait a minute—this sounds legalistic! No. When you take a second look you see that obedience is the fruit of faith. Read John 15. Put the two together. If obedience or disobedience is the great question at the end, but obedience is the fruit of faith, then the conclusion is obvious. There is no point in talking about fruit if we ignore from whence fruit comes. So genuine faith or false faith will be the crucial question at the end. That's why in the prophecies of Revelation 14 the real issue between the mark of the beast and the seal of God is the issue of salvation by faith or salvation by works. It's the basic issue and always has been.

Well, there are those today who say, "Wait a minute. We can't obey. The Bible teaches that we can't obey." I heard someone use a couple of texts to try to prove it. One was Romans 7:19, in the middle of Paul's statement on the Christian life: "The good that I would I do not: but the evil which I would not, that I do."

Would you use that to prove that it is impossible to obey? What about Paul's other statements on the subject, such as Romans 8:37: "We are more than conquerors"? What about the comment in Hebrews 13:20, 21? Let's read it: "Now the God of peace, that brought again from the dead our Lord Jesus, that great shepherd of the sheep, through the blood of the everlasting covenant, make you perfect in every good work to do his will, working in you that which is wellpleasing in his sight, through Jesus Christ; to whom be glory for ever and ever. Amen."

Paul wrote again in 2 Corinthians 10:4, 5: "The weapons of our warfare are not carnal, but mighty through God to the pulling down of strong holds; casting down imaginations, and every high thing that exalteth itself against the knowledge of God, and bringing into captivity every thought to the obedience of Christ."

I've heard Galatians 5:17 also used by those who want to prove that God's law cannot be kept: "The flesh lusteth against the Spirit, and the Spirit against the flesh: and these are contrary the one to the other: so that ye cannot do the things that ye would." But I challenge you to read the rest of that chapter for yourself and see what Paul is talking about. Make your decision from the weight of evidence—not from one or two texts lifted from here and there.

The evidence is strong that God is going to have a people at the very end of time who don't just defend the law of God, but who keep it. They love it and obey it. They see something about the law that is so descriptive of love and that takes love out of the abstract realm, that they meditate upon it and consider it a friend rather than an enemy. There have been people in every age who have belonged to this group.

We used to live on top of a mountain north of San Francisco. At the top of that mountain was a college. Many students came with Porsches and T-Birds and other sports cars. They used to try to see how fast they could make it up and down the curvy road between the college and the bottom of the hill, seven miles away.

My wife and I found it hard to keep from becoming police officers. I'm really quite retiring by nature, but I have what my wife calls my "used-car-lot personality." More than once I took off after one of these students and followed him into a parking lot. One night a young fellow passed me on a curve, going at breakneck speed, and I followed him up to the campus. When I pulled up behind him and shined my lights in his window, he got out. He came to me and said, "What's the matter?"

I said, "Guess."

He said, "I'm sorry I insulted you."

I said, "You didn't insult me. You insulted this entire community."

I regretted that I had only my used-car-lot personality instead of a police officer there to back me up!

Well, imagine that one day you are going down the mountain and a Porsche passes you on a curve at 90 mph. It forces a little white-haired lady coming up the hill almost into the ditch. Down near the bottom of the hill you see the Porsche again, this time alongside the road, and a black-and-white car with a red light on top is parked right behind it. You say, "Oh, how I love the law. It is my meditation all the day!"

Traffic laws protect us from the killings that come from drunk drivers. The law protects little old ladies who are driving up hills. The law can be a friend; it is based on love. When we see the law as a safeguard from a world of trouble, we begin to see why the singer of old wrote that he loved to meditate upon God's law every day. See Psalm 119:97.

There are a few safeguards we ought to include when we talk about the law of God. They are significant axioms that are always true. One, obedience to law can never produce righteousness. It is righteousness that produces obedience.

Where does righteousness come from? Not from trying to keep the law—it comes from Jesus. A person who has a faith relationship with Jesus will discover that righteousness produces obedience.

Another axiom: The question is not whether I can keep the law for acceptance with God. The question is rather, After Christ accepts me, can He give me the power to obey?

And one other—for those who are trying to do away with the law in order to find assurance today. It is wrong to give people assurance on the basis of imperfection. Only a legalist would do that. Those who are trying to do away with the law and downgrade the law in order to find assurance are advertising the fact that they are legalists. Our assurance is based upon what Jesus has done at the cross and our acceptance of His love on a continuing basis. Our assurance is based totally on Jesus—not on what we do or do not do. For those who are in the faith relationship with Jesus and whose assurance is based upon His merits, the law becomes good news, for it brings us continually to Him.

"Oh," someone says, "I can't obey; I've tried." Neither could the paralytic walk, but Jesus said, "Rise, take up your bed and walk." And he did. Someone says, "I can't obey; I've tried." Neither could Moses open the Red Sea. But he did. Someone says, "I can't obey; it's too big an order." Neither could Jonathan take his armor-bearer and climb the mountain and chase the entire enemy forces. But he did.

Someone says, "It's impossible for me to obey the law." It was impossible for Joshua to make the sun stand still. But he did. Someone says, "There's no way I can obey." Neither could Gideon wipe out the Midianites with 300 men and torches and trumpets, but they did. Someone says, "I can't keep God's law." Neither could Peter walk on water. But he did.

God expects more of us than what *we* can do. This is so, because the things that are impossible with man are possible with God. He has promised that if we give ourselves to His control, He will work in us "to will and to do of His good pleasure." Philippians 2:12, 13.

Jesus Revealed in Ten Commandments

When I was a boy my dad used to say, "Son, remember that it always pays to do right, and it never pays to do wrong." *Touché!* How could you disagree with that? But some of us have learned the hard way that even though the Ten Commandments express what is right and warn against what is wrong, there is no power in them to help us obey.

The wise man, near the close of his life, spoke of the importance of the commandments of God. Ecclesiastes 12:13, 14: "Let us hear the conclusion of the whole matter." Are you interested in what the wisest man who ever lived had to say as a conclusion to the whole business? Solomon came to the throne before he was eighteen years of age. He brought in gold from Ophir and silver from the mines of Spain. He imported precious stones and spices from Arabia and ivory from India. Ten thousand people sat at his table every day. Annually his fleets brought in resources from foreign shores amounting to ten million dollars. The Queen of Sheba came to find out about his wealth and said when she left that the half had not been told her. She gave him a present of three million dollars. Solomon lectured on natural history, zoology, and ornithology. He spoke 3000 proverbs and composed 1005 songs, yet he had to be old enough to die before he knew enough to live. After he had learned from God and from the school of hard knocks, at the end of his days he summed up the whole business. He said, "Fear God, and keep his commandments: for this is the whole duty of man. For God shall bring every work into judgment, with every secret thing, whether it be good, or whether it be evil."

Solomon recognized the value of God's commandments. His father David spoke often of God's law and composed his longest psalm to praise it. Paul, one of the greatest of the apostles, had much to say in favor of God's law and related it to his emphasis on righteousness by faith. Jesus was very friendly to the law of God. Some people thought He wasn't. Why? Because they confused God's law with tradition, and it is possible for us to make the same mistake today. Jesus made it clear in Matthew 5:17-19 that He was in favor of the law of God. Notice the wording: "Think not that I am come to destroy the law, or the prophets: I am not come to destroy, but to fulfill. For verily I say unto you, Till heaven and earth pass, one jot or one tittle shall in no wise pass from the law, till all be fulfilled. Whosoever therefore shall break one of these least commandments, and shall teach men so, he shall be called the least in the kingdom of heaven: but whosoever shall do and teach them, the same shall be called great in the kingdom of heaven."

I can remember public meetings, when I was a boy, hearing people make the contention that to *fulfill* meant "to do away with." And I can remember my preacher father reading the verse that way: "Think not I am come to destroy the law or the prophets, I am not come to destroy, but to do away with." It didn't make sense! Obviously, the word *fulfill* doesn't mean "to do away with," because when Jesus was baptized by John the Baptist, He said, "Suffer it to be so now: for thus it becometh us to fulfill all righteousness." Matthew 3:15. He didn't do away with righteousness by being baptized, He simply made it more beautiful, put His stamp of approval on it.

For a long time Seventh-day Adventists have been charged with being legalists because of our emphasis on the Ten Commandments.

Jesus was friendly to the Ten Commandments. In Matthew 22 He gave a concise breakdown of the two major sections. A lawyer asked Him which was the great commandment. Notice verses 37 to 40: Jesus said, "This is the first and great commandment," that "Thou shalt love the Lord thy God with all thy heart, and with all thy soul, and with all thy mind." "And the second is like unto it, Thou shalt love thy neighbour as thyself. On these two commandments hang all the law and the prophets." Occasionally someone says that Jesus gave just two commandments, love God and love our fellowmen. They fail to read the whole context. The Ten Commandments are arranged in two parts; the first four deal with love to God, and the last six with love to our neighbor. On these two principles the entire law is based.

Jesus was friendly to the Ten Commandments and revealed them in His life. The Ten Commandments are the character of God written out. The same things that are said about God are said about His law, and vice versa. God is truth (John 14:6), His law is truth (Psalm 119:142). God is righteous (Psalm 145:17, His law is righteous (Psalm 119:172). God is perfect (Matthew 5:48), His law is perfect (Psalm 19:7). God is holy (Isaiah 6:3), His law is holy (Romans 7:12). God is unchangeable (Malachi 3:6), the law is unchangeable (Matthew 5:18). God is spiritual (John 4:24), His commandments are spiritual (Romans 7:14). God is forever (Psalm 9:7 and 90:2), His law is forever (Psalm 119:44). Which means that it always has been, and it always will be, wrong to kill and lie and covet and steal and commit adultery and take God's name in vain. It has always been wrong; it will always be wrong. There is no time when God's law is changed.

Why? Because the Ten Commandments characterize

what God is and what Jesus is. I like the story of the woman who went to the fabric shop, looking for some material to make a dress. She rummaged through the bolts of cloth and finally found one that appealed to her. She paused, fingering the cloth, holding it up to the light, and the proprietor of the store noticed. He came to her and said, "You like that fabric?"

"Well, I think I do. I was just trying to visualize what it would look like made up into a dress."

He said, "Why, it just so happens that we have some of this same material made up into a dress on display in the front window. You must have missed it when you came in." They went to the window and looked at the dress made from the same cloth. The woman said, "In the bolt the fabric is beautiful, but made up into a dress it is even more beautiful. I'll take it."

We can look at the law of God and join David, Solomon, and Paul in recognizing the beauty of the law. Not a single improvement can be made, except for one—to see those Ten Commandments made up into a life. The principles are beautiful on tables of stone; they are much more beautiful made up into the life of Jesus, for Jesus reveals the Ten Commandments.

Some people get confused about the laws in the Bible. In the days of Moses there were at least four different kinds of laws. There were civil laws, health laws, ceremonial laws, and the Ten Commandments, or God's law. The civil laws may not always apply to our present society. The ceremonial laws ended at the cross; they were nailed to the cross in a sense, because they pointed forward to something that was to happen at the cross. This is a clue for anyone who stumbles over Colossians 2:14-16. It can be a problem if you don't distinguish carefully between the types of laws in the Old Testament.

The Ten Commandments did not point forward to some-

thing that was to come. The Ten Commandment law is
quoted by James, Paul, and Jesus. It would be hard to argue
against the fact that one of the heaviest qualifications of
God's law is the fact that He gave it from Mount Sinai with
His own voice.

Why did God give the Ten Commandments at Sinai?
What was His purpose in spelling them out in that way?
Let's notice the different purposes for law. In the first
place, the law is given for knowledge to people who have
become ignorant. Romans 3:20: "By the law is the knowledge of sin." Did Adam and Eve have the Ten Commandment law hanging on a tree somewhere in the Garden of
Eden? No, they didn't need it.

Why did God finally have to give the commandments at
Mount Sinai? He had two million illiterate people who had
forgotten most of what they ever knew because of the deg-
radation of their bondage in Egypt. The degeneration of
mankind had gone so far that God had to write His law down
so they could learn it.

My major professor used to illustrate by saying, "When I
invite you to dinner at my house, I don't hang signs on the
wall saying Don't spit! Why? I give you credit for knowing
better than to do that. But if it turned out that you didn't
know better, then I might have to put a sign on the wall."

God's law existed before it was written down, because sin
is the transgression of God's law. See 1 John 3:4. Hundreds
of years before Sinai, Joseph said, "How can I sin?" See
Genesis 39:9. Even before that, Abraham kept God's law.
See Genesis 18:19. These ancient men knew about it. But at
Mount Sinai it was written out for everyone to see clearly.

Another purpose for law is given in James 2. The law is a
standard in the judgment. James 2:10: "Whosoever shall
keep the whole law, and yet offend in one point, he is guilty
of all." Verse 12: "So speak ye, and so do, as they that shall
be judged by the *law of liberty*." Italics supplied. Some

have said that God's Ten Commandments are a yoke of bondage. But remember, God led Israel *out* of bondage to Mount Sinai, and James saw the truth clearly. Keeping God's law is liberty.

We noticed in the last chapter that the law is also for protection. When a traffic officer stops a reckless driver, it is for the protection of everyone—even the one who is driving recklessly.

Then we have the law as a schoolmaster. See Galatians 3:24. The law is used in a legitimate sense as a truant officer to bring us to the school of Christ. It is legitimate to think of the law as a standard of righteousness. It is legitimate to think of it as knowledge for ignorant people. But it is illegitimate, and always has been, to try to use the law as a method for salvation. This, of course, is the point upon which the apostle Paul was insistent.

Finally, the law of God reveals the love of God, because no one is going to be happy until he knows what the rules are. It has been demonstrated many times over in the lives of young people. In home, at school, on the playground, no young person is happy or secure until he knows what the rules are. Young people become very unhappy when the rules of a game are not clearly stated, whether it's basketball or tennis or Monopoly. If you don't have rules, you don't have a game. And if you don't understand the rules of life, you don't have a happy person. The Ten Commandments clearly, concisely and yet comprehensively state God's love for people He wants to be secure and happy.

Someone set the Ten Commandments to verse in this way:

Above all else, love God alone.
Bow down to neither wood nor stone.
God's name refuse to take in vain.
The Sabbath rest with care maintain.

Respect your parents all your days.
Hold sacred human life always.
Be loyal to your chosen mate.
Steal nothing, whether small or great.
Report with truth your neighbor's deed,
And rid your mind of selfish greed.

The Ten Commandments represent only the minimum. They are expanded throughout the rest of Scripture, and the Holy Spirit can continue to expand them in our minds and lives today. It is one thing not to steal—but the commandment can be expanded on the positive side to defend our neighbor's rights and property. The sky is the limit in greater understanding and interpretation for every one of God's Ten Commandments.

I'd like to remind you that the one who finds hostility in his heart toward the law of God is advertising something bad. Romans 8:7: "The carnal mind is enmity against God: for it is not subject to the law of God, neither indeed can be." The sinful mind, the heart that has never been renewed by God's grace, the person who has never been born again, is the one who is against God's commandments. Revelation 12:17 says that it is the dragon who is against God's commandments, and the same chapter identifies the dragon as the devil.

First John 5:2, 3 says that the commandments are not grievous. If someone says the Ten Commandments are a yoke of bondage, they are advertising a problem in their own hearts. For Jesus magnified the law and made it honorable. See Isaiah 42:21.

But it is possible to look at the law of God and see the beauty there and yet say, "Woe is me." Paul expressed this paradox in Romans 7 when he said, "I delight in the law of God after the inward man." "I consent unto the law that it is good." "For we know that the law is spiritual: but I am carnal, sold under sin." We find a problem in the law of God, that there is no power there. We are no more able to keep God's law than was the paralytic able to walk. See Luke 5:24. What can we do?

If you put an ax in the hands of a two-year-old and tell him to chop down a tree, the ax is weak through the flesh. You put the same ax in the hands of an experienced woodsman, and the tree comes crashing to the ground. God's Ten Commandment law is weak through the flesh, but when the Son of God comes in, there is a different story. Apart from Jesus it is impossible for us to obey the law of God, but we can do all things through Christ who strengthens us.

Which brings us to the next major pillar, the faith of Jesus. To study the law alone brings nothing but frustration. The faith of Jesus brings power to obey. We can be more than conquerors through Him who loved us.

The Faith of Jesus

We have noticed that the robe is just as free as is the invitation, that living the Christian life is just as much a gift as is forgiveness. We have seen that both justification and sanctification are by faith in Jesus Christ. Sometimes we use the phrase "righteousness by faith." Really, that is a misnomer. It is righteousness by faith in Jesus. Faith always has to have an object; it is never an end in itself. So justification is by faith alone in Jesus Christ, and sanctification is by faith alone in Jesus Christ.

We are going to look briefly at the faith of Jesus. In Revelation 14:12 we have a glimpse of the last people just before Jesus comes. It describes them as people who keep the commandments of God and have the faith of Jesus. That's the only way anyone can keep the commandments of God!

Some say it is impossible to obey God's commandments perfectly. They say we can obey, but not perfectly. I guess you'll have to explain that to me. Is it possible to be a little bit pregnant? It seems that in keeping the commandments of God, either you do or you don't. It's all or nothing. I don't think there is such a thing as obeying imperfectly. If my children came to me and said, "Well, I told the truth, but I didn't tell it perfectly," I'd say, "Let's see if we can't work on that one a little bit, maybe out in the back room!" Either you obey or you don't.

The only way anyone can keep the commandments of God is through the same kind of faith that Jesus had. What was Jesus' faith? It was faith or trust or dependence upon another for power instead of upon Himself. This was one of the hardest things Jesus did, because He had the power. He had power that you and I will never have. He was born with it. He was God as well as man. He was tempted all His life to use that power. But He never did. Instead, His life is an example of one who lives through dependence upon the power that comes from the Father. Jesus received it by personal communion in Bible study and prayer. The same power is available to you and me today, and we can receive it the same way—through personal communion with God in Bible study and prayer.

The next time you hear someone say that we can't obey, you probably ought to read him 2 Corinthians 10:4, 5: "The weapons of our warfare are not carnal, but mighty through God to the pulling down of strong holds; casting down imaginations, and every high thing that exalteth itself against the knowledge of God, and bringing into captivity every thought to the obedience of Christ." And Hebrews 13:20, 21: It is God's will to "make you perfect in every good work to do his will, working in you that which is wellpleasing in his sight."

There is too much Bible evidence that God has the power for us to obey, power to overcome, for us to claim that it's impossible. So if you ever hear that all we can do is just keep falling and failing and sinning until Jesus comes, you'd better check it out for yourself and see what the Bible says on the subject.

This leads to the next question. How? Let's get down to the nitty gritty, where the rubber meets the road, and put some shoes on this premise.

All true obedience comes from the heart. It comes from the inside out. See Matthew 12:33-35. If that's true, then any obedience that doesn't come from the heart has to be false obedience, right? Any external obedience, where I am forcing myself to obey, must be false obedience. "All true obedience comes from the heart. It was heart work with Christ. And if we consent, He will so identify Himself with our thoughts and aims, so blend our heart and minds into conformity to His will, that when obeying Him we shall be but carrying out our own impulses."—*The Desire of Ages,* p. 668. Do you like the sound of impulsive obedience? Would obedience be hard work if we were obeying impulsively? When we are controlled by Christ, we will say with the psalmist, "I delight to do thy will, O my God: yea, thy law is within my heart." Psalm 40:8. As one Christian writer has said, "When we know God as it is our privilege to know Him, our life will be a life of continual obedience. Through an appreciation of the character of Christ, through communion with God, sin will become hateful to us."—*The Desire of Ages,* p. 668.

Now let me ask you, If you hated sin as Jesus did (Hebrews 1:9), if your highest delight was in doing His will, if in obeying Him you were but carrying out your own impulses, would it be hard to do what's right? Would it be hard to obey? I'd like to go so far as to say it would be hard not to! Well, that certainly holds up the goal and shows us what we're shooting at. But what about when it doesn't happen?

Here's an old letter written on blue paper. It says, "Help! I have some questions I thought were answered a couple of years ago, so elementary I've hesitated to ask. Please overlook my baby-Christian ideas and tell me what you've discovered, since you've been on the route longer than I have. This business of the will: How far do we take it? Is giving God our will all we have to do?

"To clarify, here's an example. And that is all it is. It is not the problem, but the principles might apply. How does one go about fighting his appetite? Does he just tell God he can't control it, and ask God to take his will, and then let God make him not want to eat?

"In the meantime, when he is hungry, should he take diet pills to help God out? Keep busy all day long to stay away from food? Run out of the kitchen so he won't be exposed to temptation? Or just say 'God, you can do whatever you want with my will, including controlling my appetite. I can't. The results are up to you.' And then literally sit back and eat while he waits for God to change his will and actions? When God gets him to the place where he does not want to eat, because he knows it is against God's will." (That's a little weird right there; the last time I heard, God was in favor of eating!) "He does not want to hurt God; however, he still wants to eat because food tastes good. Should he go ahead and eat while he waits for God to take away the desire, or exercise his willpower and try not to? What is the relationship between will and willpower? When I ask God to wash away my sins and give me a new heart, am I to believe He does because He has promised? Then do I just wait for Him to do it all, no matter how long it takes, the don't-sweat-it, just-surrender philosophy? Does He take away the food, or the appetite? Will He answer prayers for other things while appetite indulgence continues?

"I have read a lot of answers and promises; I have experienced the solutions to many, but this time I am baffled. Maybe I am impatient or looking for an easy way out, but I think I am being honest with God and myself. How literal are the instructions and promises? I am anxious for your reply, because the hang-ups hang on."

Well, do you think that deserves an answer? I happen to know where the letter came from—from a brilliant young woman who was a minister's wife. She was a theologian in her own right. She studied theology and Greek and Hebrew and all the rest of those deep subjects. She's anxious for my reply—the letter is faded and tattered! Well, I gave her my reply in person, and I'm going to give it to you. I want to give the shortest version possible.

If you enter into a relationship with the Lord Jesus, and continue that relationship with Jesus from now until He comes, He will do the rest. That's the simplest answer. Philippians 1:6 says, "He which hath begun a good work in you will perform it until the day of Jesus Christ."

If the robe is as free as the invitation, and if, as we have already noticed, all we can do is get with Christ and stay with Christ, then the answer is very simple. Do you have a meaningful, vital relationship with the Lord Jesus? The sum and substance of the whole matter of Christian grace and experience is contained in believing in Christ, in knowing God and His Son whom He has sent. See John 17:3.

It sounds simple, but I'd like to remind you that this is the very thing most Christians are not spending enough time on. They think it is reserved for little old ladies with white hair and arthritis who are cramming for their finals. It's not for us. It's too mystical. We've got to try hard to do what's right, try hard to be good, try hard to make it. That's the very secret of our defeat. Most of us in that syndrome are very familiar with the knots on our heads. We are bruised and battered because we are doing everything except the one thing Jesus invites us to do: Come to Him, stay with Him, accept the rest and victory He is waiting to give us.

I know this carries with it some real hang-ups. I know what it's like to be reading my Bible in the morning and looking at the clock to see if I've got in my hour yet. I know what it's like to read about the life of Jesus and keep skipping ahead to see how many more pages till the end of the chapter. If you think you're the only one who has ever done that, guess again.

But when you got bogged down in your studies at school, you didn't quit school because it was hard work, did you? When I studied United States government in school, I was bored to death. I would rather have read the telephone directory. But did I quit school because I didn't like U.S. government? No, I stayed with it. I had a goal in mind that had to do with my life's career. Shouldn't we give God at least equal time with the history professor, when it has to do not only with time, but with eternity?

I believe that when we realize that Jesus is knocking at the door of the heart, it only makes sense to give Him at least equal time with the history professor.

Some of us have talked about the devotional life just enough to make some people nervous. They have said, "That's just another system of works. Don't talk about it. You're just giving us something else to do."

I was worrying about this one day when I got another letter. The writer likened the devotional experience of the Christian to Noah's ark. The letter started out, "My dear friend Noah." See if you get the message.

"My dear friend Noah,

"I have felt for some time that I should write to you in regard to some of the things you have been preaching lately. Please understand that I support you personally and believe you to be sincere. But there are several points that perhaps you should clarify. I'm quite sure you don't really believe what you appear to be saying.

"First of all, let me commend you on your message that a flood is coming. You know, of course, that I believe this as much as you do. A flood is indeed coming, and the world must be warned. I know the Lord has given you a special message on this matter, and you have preached it many times. Also, let me join you in your concern that people understand that they must look to the Lord for deliverance from the flood. It is only through His work on our behalf that we can be saved from the flood. We must look totally to Him for our salvation. We have no merits of our own that can commend us to His favor, and our assurance must always be in His merits. Perhaps you need to emphasize this more; I know you believe it.

"But this thing about an ark: Many feel you have spent far too much time talking about it. I'm afraid I'll have to agree with them, although I don't for a moment question your sincerity in doing so. Can't you see this smacks of legalism? It is, if you will forgive me, an extremely subjective approach to the problem of the flood. Our salvation cannot in any way be dependent upon anything we do. I'm afraid many people are looking to getting into the ark as just another works trip. We must never make, or even appear to make, anything we do a basis or condition for our salvation from the flood.

"I urge you to rethink your position carefully. If, by some remote chance you happen to be right about this ark, then let's face it, Noah, you're ahead of your time. If there is a chance that before the flood is over this business about an ark might become relevant, then at least wait until it has rained long enough so people can begin to judge accurately and fairly for themselves as to whether or not God expects them to swim, row, or get into some ark. And then, if necessary, come at us with your ark thing. Until then, don't rock the boat.

"Sincerely yours, Ann"

Actually there was more to her name than just Ann. Her full name was "Ann T. Diluvian"!

I realize that your personal, private life with God, your devotional experience day by day, can for you become a works trip. It takes a thief to know a thief. But there's one thing I don't do when it becomes a works trip. I don't scrap it for that reason. I go to my knees and ask God to help me with the problem. I compare notes with other Christians who are struggling, to find out what has helped them. I continue to seek God, because there is one thing God cannot do for us. God has a sacred regard for our power of choice. He cannot and will not ever seek Himself for us. He's the one who said, *"Ye* shall seek me, and find me, when *ye* shall search for me with all your heart." Jeremiah 29:13, emphases supplied. The one thing God invites us to do is to consent for His involvement in our lives by opening our heart's door to a relationship with Him day by day. He invites us to spend time getting acquainted with Him.

Well, someone says, What happens next? How does it work? Can we get scientific about it? Yes, we can. We have been told that the science of salvation is important. Experimental religion is legitimate. Let's put it together this way.

There is only one true obedience. We've noticed it already; it's the kind that comes from inside out, not outside in. This obedience is spontaneous, impulsive. It is obedience that we delight in; it isn't something that is a load on our shoulders. "When we know God as it is our privilege to know Him, our life will be a life of continual obedience." First John 3:6 is a text that has been used in this connection: "Whosoever abideth in him sinneth not." So long as we abide in Him, sin has no dominion over us.

Well, you say, that sounds good, but it doesn't sound real. Most of us are painfully aware that we are not abiding in Him yet, all of the time. So we continue to fall and fail and sin. Is this par for the course? What about the period of time while we are growing toward the constant abiding in Christ?

I'm glad for 1 John 2:1: "These things write I unto you, that ye sin not." So it's possible. Don't tell me God is playing games with us. "These things write I unto you, that ye sin not. And if any man sin, we have an advocate with the Father, Jesus Christ the righteous." They are both in that one verse—the work of God for us and the work of God in us.

Jesus said to the woman dragged to Him, "I don't condemn you." See John 8:2-11. There you have justification. Then He added, "Go, and sin no more." There you have sanctification. Both are included. "We shall often have to bow down and weep at the feet of Jesus because of our shortcomings and mistakes." But even if we are overcome by the enemy, God does not forsake us. Read *Steps to Christ*, page 64.

The Bible is full of people who often had to bow down and weep at the feet of Jesus. It's obvious that they were on-again, off-again abiding. They depended upon God's power one time and upon their own power the next.

Martha. She says, "Lord, we know that whatever You ask God, He will give it to You," even in the presence of death. A few minutes later, she says, "Don't roll away the stone! There will be a stench if you open the grave!" First she shows faith; then she shows lack of faith.

Peter. He's walking on water one moment, and he's sinking the next. One moment Peter is saying, "Thou art the Christ, the Son of the living God," and Jesus gives him good marks. Moments later he speaks foolishly, and Jesus tells him, "Get thee behind me, Satan."

Moses. He is a man of God leading two million slaves from Egypt. But he takes a stick and beats on the rock when he's been told to talk to it.

Elijah. He calls down fire from heaven, then goes to pray for rain and nothing happens. He prays again and nothing happens. Again and again and again nothing happens. He prayed seven times before the rain came, because he was drunk with power. He thought all he needed to do was snap his fingers and the rain would come. He had slipped into depending upon himself, and God couldn't answer his prayer until he again came to the end of his own resources.

Joshua. He surrounds Jericho and the walls crumble. In the very next battle, at Ai, Joshua is defeated.

You can go through the list. On-again—off-again is par for the course for growing Christians, as they learn to depend upon God more and more and upon themselves less and less. God's goal is to lead us to where we will depend upon Him all the time instead of just part of the time.

We get impatient. As we continue our relationship with Him, we begin to listen to the enemy who says, "You're not even a Christian." We get discouraged with our relationship, we stop seeking God, and we fall into the pattern we are so familiar with. That's why we need to be continually reminded of the basics. If we will draw a circle around the continued relationship with Jesus, the work He has begun He will carry forward.

Someone says, "How long will it take? Will I make it by the end of time? Listen, that's in God's department, not ours. Whatever perfection He needs to take me to is His concern. Don't get bogged down talking about perfection and about how perfect is perfect. Perfection is a very unprofitable topic, because as soon as you begin to spend very much time on perfection, your attention is going to be on yourself. I'm thankful to remind you that perfection is in God's department. If the robe is a gift just as much as the invitation, I can trust Him.

Well, you say, What about while I'm trying to grow into Jesus' image, seeking Him, letting Him do His work? Will there come a time when I can realize He has accomplished it? And who *has* accomlished it? This is one of the common questions. Who's done it? Whenever you talk about the goal that God has in mind, someone is sure to ask, Who's done it? I answer, Enoch and Elijah and Moses. Beyond that, it's none of your business who's done it!

I'm not just trying to be smart. It's none of anybody's business. Whenever you hear someone talking about his own victories and how he isn't sinning anymore, you can know there's something wrong, because the closer we get to Jesus, the less we advertise our achievements. So watch out if you are ever tempted to talk about your success and victories, or if you hear someone else advertising theirs.

Here's a poem that says it well:

A lion met a tiger as they drank beside a pool.
Said the tiger to the lion, "Why are you roaring like a fool?"
"That's not foolish," said the lion, with a twinkle in his eyes.
"They call me king of all the beasts, because I advertise."

A rabbit heard them talking, ran homeward like a streak.
He thought he'd try the lion's trick, but his roar was just a squeak.
A fox was walking by that way, had luncheon in the woods.
Moral: Never advertise, unless you have the goods.

We are not the ones who achieve perfection; it is God's work. Anyone who goes around saying, "I have done it, I have realized it, I have overcome," will soon find himself overcome by the enemy. *We* don't have the goods, so we'd better not advertise!

The closer a person comes to Jesus, the smaller he will see himself in his own eyes. You can see Jesus off in the distance. As you look at Him, He may look rather short, perhaps about your size, maybe even less. But when you come closer you realize that you are but a pebble beside a mountain, and you cry out for help in your great need.

So please don't look for a time when anybody, or when you yourself are going to be able to advertise that you've reached anything. We can only bow our heads beside the publican in the temple and say, "God be merciful to me a sinner." Luke 18:12.

Faith in the Crisis

It is a real advantage to have small winds blow before the big ones come. It is an advantage to learn to run with footmen before we try to keep up with horses.

Let's notice Matthew 7, where we have Jesus' analogy of the two different types of buildings and how they withstand storm, shaking, and wind. Verse 24: "Therefore whosoever heareth these sayings of mine, and doeth them, I will liken him unto a wise man, which built his house upon a rock: and the rain descended, and the floods came, and the winds blew, and beat upon that house; and it fell not: for it was founded upon a rock. And every one that heareth these sayings of mine, and doeth them not, shall be likened unto a foolish man, which built his house upon the sand: and the rain descended, and the floods came, and the winds blew"—a great crisis, obviously—"and beat upon that house; and it fell: and great was the fall of it."

Today there are crises of wind and flood and rain, crises of tragedy and sickness and grief that reveal what we really are, instead of what we appear to be. We've noticed a sort of spiritual schizophrenia in the realm of the Christian religion; a person can look good and be bad. Even among Jesus' disciples were some who looked as good as the rest, but when a crisis came, the difference was very clear.

We see Judas casting out devils and healing the sick. Evidently he went out with the seventy as one of Christ's special representatives. But when coins tinkled in his pocket a very different character emerged. We see Peter looking good, healing the sick and raising the dead and casting out devils, but because of the direction his self-sufficiency was leading, when the heat was on he cursed and swore.

Whether in the days of Christ or in our own, the coming of a crisis is not all bad. Crises demonstrate the love of God in allowing us to look deep into our own hearts, which are deceitful above all things and desperately wicked. We need to realize our need so we can prepare for the final events of the last days. We need to discover whether our faith is genuine, based upon right motives, or whether we have selfish reasons even for being in the church.

You see a tree in the woods. It looks good on the outside, but it's rotten inside. Nobody knows its true condition until a storm breaks and the forest giant crashes down. Some of us experienced an earthquake during our college days. It struck on a Sabbath afternoon. There was a meeting going on, and a married student with his family was in the balcony. The walls began to push in and out, and the windows looked like plastic. Without a moment's hesitation he ran from the balcony to the front lawn, while his wife and children remained in the balcony. He received a great deal of ribbing for that one. Others were strangely silent when they realized what they themselves had done. If you have ever determined that if you are in a fire you won't do foolish things like rescuing the frying pan, then when there is a fire and you discover yourself going out the door with a coat hanger, you too will be quiet when people ask what happened.

My brother and I were playing around the woodshed behind Grandma's house. We both looked the same—calm, cool, and collected. A yellow jacket stung my brother. He began to cry and scream and carry on in a way that I thought was foolish—until the yellow jacket's brother stung me. What followed was the first duet my brother and I ever sang! So I say you do not know, until it hits you, just how you will react. However, some scientists who have studied human nature take the position that every reaction in a crisis is premeditated. If this is correct, it means that in some way, our reaction in a crisis is pre-programmed. It does not represent any change. The crisis reveals what we really are. That is the point. It reveals what makes us tick; it reveals the extent of our faith. When some kind of problem hits, when some kind of tragedy comes and a person shakes his fist at God, what his anger reveals is that he was quietly shaking his fist at God all the way along—even though he may not have realized it himself.

That brings us to our point concerning the wind and rain and hailstones and earthquakes. The house does not change foundations—the house goes down. If it is not based upon solid rock before the floods come, it goes down when the floods come. It's just that simple. The conclusion is inevitable. A crisis doesn't change anybody.

It is wonderful if you have some time *after* a crisis to change. This has happened and can happen. The two disciples on their way to Emmaus were discouraged and fearful, doubting and questioning. But when they discovered the secret of their burning hearts, they were able to develop a trust and faith they had not known before. A disciple who cursed and swore by the fire was able to fall on his face and change after the crisis. The crisis didn't produce the change—it produced the thinking that led to the change.

A crisis doesn't change a person, it only reveals. Usually, especially at the beginning, a crisis leads a person to increase the direction in which he is already headed. You are climbing a mountain. You fall. When you get up, you are two or three steps ahead of where you fell, farther up. If you are going down the mountain and fall, when you get up you are two or three steps below where you fell. The crisis of falling simply increases your distance in the direction in which you are headed.

After a crisis, it is possible to realize the nature of your condition and seek for a change by allowing the Holy Spirit to do His work. It is possible, if there's time.

Now concerning the direction—up or down—we have some interesting information that clarifies the misconceptions of many young people. Some have come to me in great discouragement because they have gotten the idea that if a person does something wrong just before he dies, so that he has no time to make it right, he will be lost forever. I do not believe that. I believe rather what the little book *Steps to Christ* describes, that character is determined not by the occasional good deed or the occasional misdeed, but by the direction of the life. Read about this in *Steps to Christ,* pages 57, 58.

So if you were going to graph a person's life, it might look something like this:

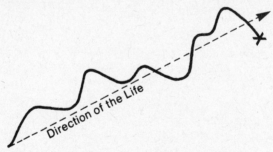

Direction of the Life

Notice that the direction of this person's life is upward, even though he dies just after losing his patience. Someone says, "Too bad, he'll never be saved." But God looks at the direction of the life.

On the other hand, you can have someone die in church, but his life looks like this:

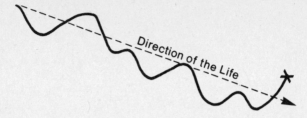

Friends may say, "Good for him! He died in church!" But where a person dies is not the deciding factor, because God looks at the direction of the life.

A crisis will often tell us the direction we are going by revealing ourselves to ourselves and also by increasing our momentum.

I do not believe very strongly in death-bed repentances. I don't know how anyone could, for if there's ever a crisis, it's death, when time and eternity meet. If a crisis simply reveals what you already are, and if a crisis does not change you, and if—as at death—there's no time after the crisis to change, how could you allow for death-bed repentances except in extremely rare exceptions?

Courage, fortitude, and trust in God do not come in a moment. These heavenly graces are acquired through the experience of years. It takes time to transform the human into the divine. So we can see that crises demonstrate the love of God. He allows the smaller winds to blow so we can see ourselves and prepare for the greater winds to come.

It is interesting to note that every temptation is a crisis, for each temptation reveals to us in its results exactly what we were at the time of temptation.

I'll never forget a comment one of my major professors made in a Bible class in seminary—that if a person is not surrendered to God at the time of the temptation, there's little chance of surrendering then. If a person doesn't already know a vital relationship with God and a dependence upon His power when the temptation comes, there's little chance of surrendering then. What usually happens is that we're on our own, depending on our own steam, our own backbone. The strong "make it," and the weak don't.

Hebrews 4:16, 17 says we have a great High Priest and that we are invited to "come boldly unto the throne of grace, that we may obtain mercy, *and* find grace to help in time of need." Italics supplied. Notice the sequence. The text does not say, "Let us come boldly unto the throne of grace in time of need." It says, "Let us come boldly unto the throne of grace, that we may obtain mercy, *and* find grace to help in time of need." The person who comes before the throne only in time of need is not going to get much grace. Have you discovered that? Grace must be found ahead of time. If grace is obtained then, the crisis of temptation will reveal its presence in your life. If grace has not been found before the crisis, the crisis will reveal its absence.

We may live so close to God day by day that in every unexpected trial our thoughts will turn to Him as naturally as the flower turns to the sun. I want that, don't you?

There are all kinds of crises. Inheriting a million dollars from a rich uncle could be a crisis. There are people who have said, "If I had lots of money, I would send ten students to school. I would build a new church. I would give this much here and that much there." They have discovered when they inherited that much money that they did nothing of the kind. I was talking to two men who came into a great sum of money, and I said impulsively, "Well, you have a real advantage. You can have your time of trouble before the rest of us. You will be able to discover what really makes you tick before the rest of us do."

I've come across a few people who think it would have been thrilling to live in the days of the martyrs. They have said to me, "If I had lived back there, with the blood of the martyrs somehow coursing through my veins, I would have just walked up to those people and said, 'You can burn me. I will not give up my faith.' " But we never know what we will do until the crisis actually comes. Many who have thought they could weather the storms on a thousand seas have drowned in a bathtub, as it were. That's the way it goes. We are so deceived concerning our own hearts. It isn't any wonder that God in His love allows trials and tribulations so we can see ourselves as we really are. No wonder James says, "Count it all joy when ye fall into divers temptations; knowing this, that the trying of your faith worketh patience. But let patience have her perfect work, that ye may be perfect and entire, wanting nothing." James 1:2, 3.

We know this much: At the very end of time, just before Jesus comes again, there will be a great crisis. People will go one way or the other *fast*. The thing that will be different about this last great crisis, when the wind blows in hurricane force, is that there will be no time afterward for change. The changes must come before that time. If that's true, then God would be exceedingly anxious to have us understand ourselves as we are, long before that time ever comes.

In Amos 8 is a prediction of a time when people will be running from sea to sea, from coast to coast, looking for an experience which they have neglected and which they can no longer find. They beat their chests and throw their riches to moles and bats. They are desperate. Many who have been called religious people will be among them—but no spiritual people, because spiritual people know God.

In the same chapter as Jesus' analogy of the two types of houses, one on rock and one on sand, He gives a clue as to how to meet the crises when they come and how to prepare for them ahead of time. There are two clues: Matthew 7:21: "He that doeth the will of my Father which is in heaven," and Matthew 7:23: "I never knew you: depart from me." Here are two factors—doing God's will and knowing Him.

This can get rather tricky because of the potential for

spiritual schizophrenia in which a person can deceive himself into thinking he's doing God's will simply because he is conforming outwardly to the standards of the church. People in Christ's day deceived themselves into thinking they were doing God's will because they paid tithe and kept the Sabbath and were careful health reformers—but all the time they were planning murder in their hearts. It is also possible for people to deceive themselves if they are depending upon their feelings. People can even cast out devils and do wonderful things in Jesus' name and still not know Him. See Matthew 7:21-23.

Therefore, it is important that we spell this out for all to understand. When we really know God as it is our privilege to know Him, our life will be a life of obedience. See 1 John 2:4. This places knowing God as the cause, and doing God's will as the result. Therefore, the more important of the two would be to know God.

One day someone said to me, "Faith and works are like two oars. You use them as two oars as you row your boat toward the celestial shores." Well, faith and works *are* like two oars in that both are needed. But they are *not* like two oars in the sense that both cause our salvation. We can say that faith and works are both important. We can say that doing God's will and knowing God are equally vital. But that still allows for the premise that one is completely the cause of the other.

So how can I know if I am headed in the right direction, if I am going toward God, if I am going up the mountain instead of down? The determining factor is, Do I have a personal, meaningful relationship of knowing God day by day?

When I know Him as it is my privilege to know Him, my life will be a life of continuous obedience. If I am having trouble with continuing obedience, I must not forget that it is *not* because I'm not trying hard enough to obey. It's because I don't yet know God as it is my privilege to know

Him. That's where the trouble is. If I will continue to get acquainted with God He has promised to complete the work that He has started. He will bring me into the final great crisis, prepared and ready to pass through it successfully. He won't brainwash me; the change will not be external. I will be a new person inside and out—the same all the way through.

During World War II agents were being trained in England in the dangerous skills of "spy and counterspy." The training camp was extremely rigorous. The teachers took the Allied troups who were going into espionage and would change their environment, change their food, change their habits and practices and customs. They dressed these soldiers in German uniforms and gave them German names. They fed them German food and taught them German expressions. They wanted them to be so completely transformed that they would consider themselves, consciously and subconsciously, to be Germans. That kind of change is hard to accomplish, when man can deal only with externals. But the leaders achieved a degree of success. Just how much success was determined by the final test which none of the trainees anticipated.

At the end of their training, they were taken out on bivouac. After marching all day and far into the night over many miles at a breakneck pace, they were finally allowed to crumple into pathetic little heaps in their pup tents. Suddenly the sergeants shook them awake. Shining spotlights into their eyes, they yelled, "Who are you?"

Now if you were one of these agents, and you blinked your sleepy eyes and said, "I'm Henry Smith"; and "Where are you from?" "From Canada"; and "Where are you going?" "Home to mother!" it wouldn't be long until you were going home to mother—or back to the battle front.

But if you awoke from your deep sleep with your training fully intact, and when they said, "Who are you?" you replied, "Mein Name ist Heinrich Schmidt"; "Where are you from?" "Ich komme von Frankfurt"; "Where are you going?" "Ich gehe nach Hamburg," it wouldn't be long until you were spying on the Germans in Hamburg.

Some passed the test. But I think I see a different scene. I see a Master Teacher who deals not simply with German black bread and clothes and expressions, not merely with outward actions. I see a Teacher who deals with minds and hearts and purposes and motives, tastes, inclinations, ambitions, passions. And because of this training in close connection with this Master Teacher, who is also our best Friend, we are transformed within and without.

Someday the spotlights come on. We are shaken as from a deep sleep. Voices demand, "Who are you?"

We reply with confidence, "I am a follower of Jesus."

"Where are you from?"

"I am a stranger and pilgrim in the earth."

"Where are you going?"

"I look for a heavenly city whose builder and maker is God."

I believe that God is determined to have every one of us among that group, don't you?

If God chooses to allow some lesser winds to blow, even if they look like big ones at the time, we can be grateful instead of fearful. For the smaller crises help us to understand ourselves so that we can, by His grace, be certain of our direction. Thank God for the little crises that prepare us for the bigger ones! Thank God that Peter had time to go down on his face in the garden and repent of his cursing and swearing and self-sufficiency. Thank God that the door of His mercy is still open to us and that today He invites us to continue to choose to go His direction, with Him. He has promised to bring us off more than conquerors through His love and power.

A Day to Remember—I

Johnny started out for Sunday School one bright, sunny day. He had two dimes in his pocket, one for the Lord and one for an ice-cream cone on his way home. He tripped at the corner, and one of the dimes went rolling down the drain out of sight. He was just regretting the loss of the Lord's dime when he met a friend who wasn't going to Sunday School. He said to Johnny, "Let's go fishing." Johnny said, "I can't go fishing. I'm going to Sunday School."

But it was such a lovely day and his friend was so persuasive, that Johnny decided to go fishing instead. He tried to time things so that he would be home about the same time as usual, but he was a little late. There was mud on his shoes, dampness on his pants, and the unmistakable odor of fish on his hands. In just a few minutes Mother had the whole story.

She said, Johnny, I'll teach you to go fishing on Sunday. I want you to go up to your room and take your Bible and read the fourth commandment fifty times."

So Johnny went up to his room and sat down and began to read. "Remember the Sabbath day, to keep it holy. Six days shalt thou labour, and do all thy work: but the seventh day is the Sabbath of the Lord thy God." He read right on through to the end and put a mark on a piece of paper. Then he read the passage again and again. Before long he had it memorized. He went through it fifty times, then came out of his room and promised his mother he would never again go fishing on Sunday.

Several weeks later, at school, the teacher said, "Today we are going to take a look at the days of the week. Who would like to give us the days of the week in order?"

Johnny raised his hand. He recited, "Monday, Tuesday, Wednesday, Thursday, Friday, Saturday, Sunday."

The teacher said, "That's fine, Johnny, except for one little problem. You started with Monday, and you should start with Sunday, the first day of the week. Would you like to try again?"

Johnny paused for a moment and started again. "Monday, Tuesday, Wednesday, Thursday, Friday, Saturday, Sunday."

The teacher said, "Pardon me, Johnny. Maybe you didn't understand. I asked you to start with the first day of the week—Sunday. Try it one more time."

There was a longer pause this time, and then Johnny came out with, "Monday, Tuesday, Wednesday, Thursday, Friday, Saturday, Sunday."

At this point the teacher told Johnny to stay after school, to which he replied, "Teacher, if you had read the fourth commandment as many times as I have, you'd *know* that Sunday is the seventh day of the week." The teacher sent Johnny home to mother for some better answers.

We've noticed that there are six major pillars that distinguish Seventh-day Adventists from other evangelical Christians: We have studied the three angels' messages, the sanctuary and judgment, the law of God and the faith of Jesus. Now we take a look at the Sabbath pillar. In the next chapters we will look at the condition of mankind in death. These are the landmarks, or what our pioneers considered the basic pillars of our faith.

We have noticed two threads running through all these

pillars. One is justification by faith, the great teaching of Martin Luther and the Reformation. The other is sanctification by faith, for which John Wesley was well known. We find an interesting combination of these two in all our pillars.

As we consider the Sabbath pillar, I invite you to read from a familiar chapter. Notice particularly the reason given in the middle of Exodus 20:8-11 as to *why* the Sabbath should be kept. "Remember the sabbath day, to keep it holy. Six days shalt thou labour, and do all thy work: but the seventh day is the sabbath of the Lord thy God: in it thou shalt not do any work, thou, nor thy son, nor thy daughter, thy manservant, nor thy maidservant, nor thy cattle, nor thy stranger that is within thy gates." *"Why?* "For in six days the Lord made heaven and earth, the sea, and all that in them is, and rested the seventh day: wherefore the Lord blessed the sabbath day, and hallowed it."

When did the Sabbath begin? At creation. So the idea that you may have heard that the Sabbath was made for the Jewish people doesn't hold up, because the Jewish people consider Abraham the father of their race, and he didn't come along for 2,000 years after the Sabbath was initiated by God. Notice that the Sabbath was in honor of the creation of the world.

Did you know that the weekly cycle has never been broken from the days of creation? The calendar has been changed, as far as the numbers, but the weekly cycle has never been broken. Did you know that there is no astronomical reason for the week, as there is for the month, the day, and the year? The only reason for the existence of the week is creation—the seven days of creation.

Our pioneers in the middle of the last century came across the Sabbath truth after it had been largely lost sight of for centuries. These early advent believers had listened to the Baptist preacher, William Miller, and believed that Jesus was coming back in 1844. He didn't return and they were disappointed. But those who continued to study found the answer to their disappointment in the teachings of the sanctuary and judgment, as we have already noticed. As they studied the sanctuary described in the Old Testament, they went through the courtyard into the first apartment and the second apartment, and they came to the ark. Inside the ark they found the Ten Commandments. And included in the Ten Commandments they found the fourth commandment that made very clear which day was God's day of worship.

As they took a longer look, they discovered that the people at the very end, just before Jesus comes, are to be known by the faith of Jesus and by keeping all of the commandments. They are going to be known by their patience. They began to try to see how the Sabbath commandment fitted in with the three angels' messages that we've been studying.

About this time, Rachel Oakes, a Seventh-day Baptist, came to the town of Washington, New Hampshire. She talked to these pioneers even before 1844, trying to communicate to them about the seventh-day Sabbath, but she got little response from them. They were too engrossed in preparing for the coming of the Lord. But when the Lord didn't come they began to listen to what she was saying.

Let's think for a moment how ironic this was. Suppose Rachel Oakes, a good Christian, had come to town with the truth that you're not supposed to steal, or you're not supposed to lie and cheat, or you're not supposed to commit adultery, or one of the other commandments, and the people said, "Sorry, Rachel. We don't have time to listen to you. We're busy getting ready for the coming of the Lord." It would be almost funny, wouldn't it? But the commandment she was involved with is just as much a part of the Ten Commandments as the others.

Well, after the disappointment in 1844, broken hearts

were wide open for more truth. A man by the name of Frederick Wheeler, a Methodist preacher, listened to Rachel Oakes, accepted the Sabbath, and began to talk about it. Then a man by the name of William Farnsworth, who is buried today in the little cemetery behind the Washington, New Hampshire church, accepted the Sabbath late in 1844. Then a Baptist preacher named Thomas Preble accepted the Sabbath and began to write about it. He included in his writings some interesting warnings from Daniel 7 about a power that would try to change God's law. A retired sea captain, Joseph Bates, read Preble's writings, saw the truth, and accepted the seventh-day Sabbath. He began to write as well. And not too far away, a young couple, James and Ellen White, read Bates's writings. They accepted the Sabbath teaching as well. That was the beginning.

As these people studied the sanctuary and judgment, the ark of God and the Ten Commandments, many things began to come clear—especially as they studied the last-day events in relationship to the Sabbath.

They began to see that the Sabbath had special significance for God's people living on the earth in the last days. They realized there would come a time of test on this truth. And as they studied the prophecies of Daniel and Revelation, they saw not only that the seventh-day Sabbath is clearly taught in the Bible, but they began to realize how God feels about it, especially as they read the warnings in the message of the third angel in Revelation 14:9-12. They came to the conclusion that in the great final conflict between sin and righteousness, the law of God would be at stake, particularly the Sabbath.

Then some of them began to see something deeper than just a day of worship, for the Sabbath is a sign of salvation by faith. In the day of worship that the anti-Christ power of Daniel and Revelation introduced, they discovered a symbol of salvation by works.

So the deeper issue involved is faith or works, God's method of salvation against the devil's system. It became an issue of faith in God or in your own efforts. It became an issue of rest, or an issue of labor. And it included the issue of loyalty to God, because the Sabbath, as they discovered, is the birthday of the world, a day every week in honor of creation. Not even God Himself can change the birthday of the world. Nobody can change anyone's birthday.

Let's say that your birthday is in July, but I decide that I'm going to change your birthday to November 1 this year. I tell you, "Your birthday is now changed to November 1." You say, "Who do you think you are, anyway? God Himself can't change my birthday!"

Even the people who tried to change Lincoln's birthday and Washington's birthday have to admit they didn't succeed. I understand that Lincoln was still born on the same date he was born on. So now we have a day called "Presidents' Day." It only proves one thing. The birthdays haven't been changed. The fact that such a change was attempted is proof that Lincoln and Washington just aren't that important to us anymore.

So it is foolish, as well as blasphemous, for this anti-Christ power of Daniel and Revelation to think it can change God's law involving the birthday of the world.

Well, as these people continued to study, they realized that there would be a group of God's people at the very end of time who would rather die for truth than give it up, who would rather die for Christ and His law than give them up. According to Revelation 13 and Daniel 7, that is exactly what the issues will be. There will be a great deal of trouble created for God's people concerning their loyalty to Him and His law.

Let's stop here for a moment. Suppose I was one of these people who say that God's law cannot be obeyed. If that were true, no one would be able to obey the Sabbath commandment, right? Why would anyone die for truth that cannot be obeyed?

Let's substitute: Instead of the Sabbath commandment in the middle of the ten, suppose that someone hauled you into court someday because they wanted to force you to steal. Suppose the "mark of the beast" was forcing everyone to steal, to break the eighth command instead of the fourth. They bring you to court and say, "We understand that you believe God's law says you shouldn't steal."

You say, "Yes, that's what I believe."

They say, "We are going to force everyone to steal, and if you refuse to steal, you will be killed."

You say, "Why, I don't believe that law can be *kept*."

They say, "I beg your pardon?"

You say, "I don't believe it's possible to keep that commandment about not stealing. In fact, I'm a kleptomaniac myself."

They say, "Pardon me. Evidently we got you into court by mistake!" They dismiss your case at once.

Why would anyone haul you into court to force you to break a law you don't believe can be kept? Would it make sense? Yet the prediction in both Daniel and Revelation is that people will be called before the court concerning the Sabbath, the fourth commandment.

Would you die for a commandment you were failing on all the time? The Bible teaches that if you know what it means to have the faith of Jesus, then you have power available to obey God's law. Those who defend God's law are not just watching over and guarding it; they believe and experience the power of God to obey it.

Well, all of this made sense to the early pioneers. They began to be great defenders of the law and the Sabbath. They talked so much about the law and the Sabbath that they began to neglect the cross and forgiveness. They tended to take it for granted that everyone in the Christian world knew about the cross and forgiveness, so they neglected the foundation of the Christian faith, the atonement, and Jesus who died for our sins, because they were too busy defending the law and the Sabbath.

As we neared the end of the last century, a little lady in their midst wrote to the church and said, "We have preached the law until we are as dry as the hills of Gilboa that had neither dew nor rain. We must preach Christ in the law, and there will be sap and nourishment in the preaching that will be as food to the famishing flock of God."—E. G. White, *Review and Herald,* March 11, 1890.

Now I'd like to shift gears for a moment and suggest something that would be worth a whole book sometime. It's found in Hebrews 4, and the key word is *rest*. When you think of the Sabbath, do you think of rest? Evidently the writer of this passage thought of rest. Even though this chapter takes a little extra study, there is something there that we're overdue in understanding.

God has in mind that we rest in three ways—that we rest from trying to earn our way to heaven, that we rest from trying to overcome the enemy and obey God's law through our own efforts, and that we rest from thinking we can get to the Promised Land by ourselves. Salvation is *all* God's work.

Hebrews 4 discusses the Jewish people, and why Israel wandered in the wilderness for so long before entering the Promised Land. The reason was their lack of faith. These people did not enter into God's rest even though they were God's people. When Moses went into Egypt and faced Pharaoh, he said, "Thus saith the Lord, Let my people go." So they were God's people. Through all their wilderness wanderings, they offered sacrifices morning and evening. They had the lambs that pointed to Jesus. God was with them. But here in the book of Hebrews, we can take note of a message that was written for us today.

Hebrews 4:4: "He spake in a certain place of the seventh day on this wise, And God did rest the seventh day from all his works." Then there is a plea to us to enter into God's rest. Notice verses 9 and 10: "There remaineth therefore a rest to the people of God, for he that is entered into his rest, he also hath ceased from his own works, as God did from his."

Now you might think at first glance this chapter is talking about the rest from trying to earn your way to heaven. Well, that's included in the chapter in verse 3, where the last phrase tells us that the works were finished from the foundation of the world. There is a similar phrase in Revelation 13:8 about the Lamb slain from the foundation of the world. So justification is suggested briefly in this chapter. But the main thrust of the chapter is sanctification, resting from our own efforts to be victorious. The Sabbath is given as a symbol of this.

Now notice that the Sabbath, as well as being a memorial of creation was to be a symbol of sanctification. If you want to check that out, read Ezekiel 20:12, 20 and Exodus 31:13. So when Hebrews 4 talks about the Sabbath rest, it is talking about the rest involved in sanctification. When we think of sanctification, we think of living the Christian life. Let me ask you, Do you find living the Christian life a restful thing? Or do you find it hard work? Have you exchanged the burden of sin for the burden of holiness? Have you discovered meaning in Jesus' gracious invitation, "Come unto me, all ye that labour and are heavy laden, and I will give you rest"?

Have you experienced the rest that Christ gives, not only from the guilt of sin but from its power? Or are you still trying hard to obey God's law? When we come to Jesus for rest and He gives us the power that we don't have, we can find obedience restful.

Even to this very day, the words of Hebrews 4 still ring in

the ears of God's people—there still remains a rest to the people of God.

Then in verse 11 we read something that may seem hard to understand: "Let us labour therefore to enter into that rest." How do you labor to rest? The two words fight each other! Well, let's go back to Jesus' invitation in Matthew 11, "Come unto me, all ye that labour and are heavy laden, and I will give you rest." If we have rest by coming to Him, and if we are to labor to rest, then the labor would have to be the effort put forth day by day to come to Jesus.

Have you found that it takes effort to reserve the prime time of your day to spend alone with God? I have discovered that at times it takes every bit of effort I can produce. It may be even harder for preachers, because it is easy for us to become so busy about the work of the Lord that we forget the Lord of the work.

But in your workaday schedule, it can take real planning and backbone and determination—labor—to come to Christ personally, alone, day by day. That's where the labor is, in coming to Him and in continuing to come to Him. But that's the way we enter into rest, and that's the way the Sabbath becomes meaningful.

"Oh," you may say, "I don't need the Sabbath. I can have a special time for communion with God any day of the week." No, even though we spend time in communion with Christ every day, we are still promised that Jesus will come in a special way on the seventh day. He's been doing it ever since creation.

All these things became clear to our pioneers, and even though Adventists today are not interested in keeping the Sabbath just to be different, they are willing to put up with comments from people who don't understand, because they see something far deeper in this day of worship which involves their Creator, their Lord, their Saviour, and their Friend.

A Day to Remember—II

Seventh-day Adventists have been accused of getting on the beast and riding it with spurs, and for good reason. We have even been in danger of learning to hate the beast more than loving Jesus. I hope that in the process of taking a brief look at Daniel and Revelation on this issue we can somehow see the love and image of Jesus more than the image to the beast.

Let's begin with Revelation 14:1: "I looked, and, lo, a Lamb stood on the mount Sion, and with him an hundred and forty and four thousand, having his Father's name written in their foreheads. And I heard a voice from heaven, as the voice of many waters, and as the voice of a great thunder: and I heard the voice of harpers harping with their harps: and they sung as it were a new song before the throne, and before the four beasts, and the elders: and no man could learn that song but the hundred and forty and four thousand, which were redeemed from the earth. These are they which were not defiled with women; for they are virgins. These are they which follow the Lamb whithersoever he goeth. These were redeemed from among men, being the firstfruits unto God and to the Lamb. And in their mouth was found no guile: for they are without fault before the throne of God."

This group of people have the Father's name written in

their foreheads. They are a group who are extremely loyal to the end of the great controversy between good and evil. The same group is also mentioned in Revelation 7:1-4: "After these things I saw four angels standing on the four corners of the earth, holding the four winds of the earth, that the wind should not blow on the earth, nor on the sea, nor on any tree. And I saw another angel ascending from the east, having the seal of the living God: and he cried with a loud voice to the four angels, to whom it was given to hurt the earth and the sea, saying, Hurt not the earth, neither the sea, nor the trees, till we have sealed the servants of our God in their foreheads. And I heard the number of them which were sealed: and there were sealed an hundred and forty and four thousand of all the tribes of the children of Israel."

Foreheads again. The spotlight is on foreheads. Here you have a group of people sealed in their foreheads; the Father's name is written in their foreheads. Obviously, they're on God's side.

Now there's another group that gets something in their foreheads. You can read about them in Revelation 13:1-9. Let's notice the entire passage so we have our setting straight before we go on. "I stood upon the sand of the sea, and saw a beast rise up out of the sea, having seven heads and ten horns, and upon his horns ten crowns, and upon his heads the name of blasphemy. And the beast which I saw was like unto a leopard, and his feet were as the feet of a bear, and his mouth as the mouth of a lion: and the dragon gave him his power, and his seat, and great authority. And I saw one of his heads as it were wounded to death; and his deadly wound was healed: and all the world wondered after the beast. And they worshipped the dragon which gave power unto the beast: and they worshipped the beast, saying, Who is like unto the beast? who is able to make war with him? And there was given unto him a mouth speaking great things and blasphemies; and power was given unto him to continue forty and two months. And he opened his mouth in blasphemy against God, to blaspheme his name, and his tabernacle, and them that dwell in heaven. And it was given unto him to make war with the saints, and to overcome them: and power was given him over all kindreds, and tongues, and nations. And all that dwell upon the earth shall worship him, whose names are not written in the book of life of the Lamb slain from the foundation of the world. If any man have an ear, let him hear."

Later, this chapter talks about a power that will give life to this beast. Verse 16: "He causeth all, both small and great, rich and poor, free and bond, to receive a mark in their right hand, or in their foreheads: and that no man might buy or sell, save he that had the mark, or the name of the beast, or the number of his name."

So here you have the other group that emerge at the end of the great conflict between good and evil. They are followers of the beast, and they have something of the beast in their foreheads—a mark—not a seal, but a mark. So the contrast at the end of time is between two groups, one with the seal of God and the name of God in their foreheads, and the other with the mark of the beast in their foreheads or *in their hand.* A very interesting addition.

I wish there were some way of making this subject simple, down to earth, so that the smallest boy and girl who can comprehend at all could understand. Let's try.

When Jesus comes again, you will have either the name of God in your forehead or the mark of the beast in your forehead or hand. Two choices. Obviously these two groups will have polarized out of more than two groups, because up until shortly before Jesus comes there will be at least three groups. Revelation 3 talks about them, the hot, the cold, and the lukewarm.

But when Jesus actually comes, the three groups will

have turned into two groups, only two. Lukewarm has disappeared, and there are only hot and cold. There will be those with the seal of God in their foreheads, and those with the mark of the beast in their forehead or hand. Other labels include the good and the bad, the righteous and the wicked, the wheat and the tares, the sheep and the goats.

Do you have a pretty good idea which group you want to be in? Do you realize the alternatives? If you are in one group, you're not going to be able to buy or sell. You will have the death penalty on you. This is God's group. If you're in the other group, you will experience something called the seven last plagues; you're going to gnaw your tongue with pain, the sun is going to scorch you, and you will suffer a number of other things that don't sound at all desirable. When you look at the alternatives, it seems as though you are in trouble either way, doesn't it? It looks as if there will be no place to hide. But before we are finished, we will see that there is a very great difference between the two.

I'm going to give two or three points that I'm not going to try and prove. The first is that Revelation 12 talks about a power that is clearly identified as pagan or heathen Rome. The next point is in Revelation 13, where we've already read about a beast that eventually has a mark. This power gets its authority from pagan Rome. If you put together the books of Daniel and Revelation and study particularly Daniel 7 and Revelation 13, you'll find at least 8 clues that clearly identify this beast power. Here's the list: (1) This beast gets its authority from pagan Rome. (2) This beast is a blasphemous power against God. (3) It has political strength in history. (4) It makes war on God's people; we can call it a persecuting power. (5) It rules for 1260 years. (6) It receives a deadly wound at the end of that time. (7) It has a number applied to it, 666. And (8) It has a mark that people can receive in either their forehead or their right hand.

We have already noticed that God has a seal you can receive in your forehead but not in your hand. You know that the book of Revelation is full of symbols. When you receive something in your forehead, what are you receiving? Is someone going to come along with a hot iron such as cattle are branded with and press it into your forehead? No. God's seal is a symbol of something you accept into your thinking.

The human brain is made up of three parts, the cerebellum, the cerebrum and the medulla oblongata. The cerebrum is in the front of the brain, at the forehead. It is the area of the brain that is unique to man. Brute creation doesn't have much cerebrum. This is the area where conscience and reason reside. It is where God communicates with mankind. It is also the first part of the brain that is damaged by stimulants, narcotics, or intemperance. When you speak of your forehead, you are referring to your thinking processes. If you have the seal of God in your forehead, you have accepted something into your thinking, your reasoning, your conscience.

What would the right hand refer to (except for you left-handed people!)? It suggests work, action, activity. When you accept the seal of God, it has to be in your forehead. But when you accept the mark of the beast, it can be either in your forehead or in your hand. Evidently there will be some who accept the mark of the beast into their thinking, while others simply go along with it outwardly.

What is the seal of God? What is any seal? Well, the seal of a government includes at least three things. A good example is the early seal of the United States of America. It had the name of George Washington, our first ruler. It had his title, President. And it had the territory over which he ruled, the United States of America. Three parts to a seal.

Where in the Bible do you find something that spells out the name of God, His title, and the territory over which He rules? Let's look first at Revelation 14:7. This has to do with the angel that flies through the sky with a particular message just before Jesus comes again. It says, "Fear God, and give glory to him; for the hour of his judgment is come: and worship him that made heaven, and earth, and the sea, and the fountains of waters." Does that last phrase remind you of anything?

In our last chapter we considered God's day of worship, and we noticed the fourth commandment, right in the middle of God's law. Let's take another look at it. "Remember the sabbath day, to keep it holy. Six days shalt thou labour, and do all thy work: but the seventh day is the sabbath of the Lord thy God." There you have a name, right? The sabbath is the sabbath *of the Lord* thy God. "In it thou shalt not do any work, thou, nor thy son, nor thy daughter, thy manservant, nor thy maidservant, nor thy cattle, nor thy stranger that is within thy gates. For in six days the Lord made. . . . " What is His title here? Our Creator. "The Lord made." So you have His name and His title. He is the Lord, our Creator, our Maker. How much did He make? What's the territory over which He rules? He made "heaven and earth, the sea, and all that in them is." This description of God was not only given back at the time of Moses and the Jewish people, but is repeated again in Revelation 14, just before the Bible closes. In both cases you find scenes of great importance attached to the seal of God.

So we notice that the Sabbath commandment contains the seal of God, because that's where His name, His title, and the territory over which He rules show up. When you have a group of people at the very end who have the seal of God in their foreheads, they surely must be keeping the Sabbath of the fourth commandment.

But please remember, my friend, that there is more to keeping the Sabbath than being a Saturday keeper. It is possible to go through the forms and motions and attempt to get the seal of God in your hand only. But it is a futile attempt, for the seal of God is given only in the forehead. The people who truly worship God worship Him from within.

It is possible to go along with the crowd and worship the beast simply by routine and form and going through motions. You can get the mark of the beast in your forehead or in your hand. But God's seal is given only in the forehead.

All right, then, if the seal of God in the foreheads of God's people at the very end has to do with the fourth commandment and a day of worship in honor of the Creator, then the mark of the beast, which is received in the forehead or the hand, would logically have to do with a day of worship as well. But may I suggest that both of these days have to do with something deeper than just which day one should attend church. There's something far more than that.

We noticed in our study of the three angels of Revelation 14 that two threads go through all three messages—a warning against self-worship and an invitation to worship God. Let's look at a couple of Scripture passages. The first, Matthew 11:28: Jesus said, "Come unto me, all ye that labour and are heavy laden, and I will give you rest." So if a person does not have rest, it is because he is not coming to Jesus.

Couple with that Revelation 14:9-11: Those who worship the beast and his image and receive his mark, "have no rest day nor night." So if Jesus says to come to Him for rest and those who receive the mark of the beast have no rest, then the people who worship the beast and his image and receive his mark, must not be coming to Jesus. That's what the mark of the beast and the image to the beast are all about. It's about not coming to Jesus.

Now let me ask you something. Would it be possible to sit on a church pew and believe in warning the world concerning the beast and his image and mark, and still be a victim of the beast and his image and mark yourself? When we take surveys and discover that three out of four church members have no time to come to Jesus day by day, then we are sadly aware that many are being caught in the very trap they have been warning other people away from.

Don't limit the beast and his image and his mark only to a day of worship. There is something deeper. The Sabbath becomes, by the same token, a symbol of those who are in vital relationship with Jesus. In coming to Him they find rest. They look forward to the hours of the Sabbath as a special reminder of that rest Jesus offers to those who come to Him. The Sabbath becomes a symbol of sanctification and the fact that Jesus offers us rest from all our guilt and evil propensities.

Many are aware of the fact that the seventh-day Sabbath is taught in Scripture, and that according to Scripture there is nothing to support the first day of the week as a day of worship. But many of these same people have never known how God felt about it. The reason God feels so deeply is that He gave the day of worship in the first place to remind His creatures of their Creator.

If I were the devil and saw a day every week given in honor of the One who made me, I would do everything I could to get rid of it. I couldn't stand to see a day set aside to honor Him when I wanted everyone to worship me.

If you were to go to heathen lands and tell those who worship the sun that you have a God who created the sun, they would say, "Then He must be greater than our sun." If you added to that the fact that our God created not only the sun, but the earth and sea and heavens and all that in them is, including you and me, then you can't get a greater God than that. And if I were the devil and determined to exalt myself above the Most High, it would be at the top of my priority list to do away with this day of worship that honors the One who made everything.

So in the books of Daniel and Revelation you have the record that the devil has tried to change something. Here is time-of-the-end information about what will happen, how it will be attempted, and how God feels about it, and about the two groups that will emerge just before Jesus returns.

You are also faced with how Jesus feels about His law and the day of worship that He created, and about what the devil has tried to do to God's law and His day of worship. You also see how He feels about the two groups of people, those who go along with this beast power and those who remain loyal to God to the very end.

Revelation 15:2, 3: "I saw as it were a sea of glass mingled with fire: and them that had gotten the victory over the beast, and over his image, and over his mark, and over the number of his name, stand on the sea of glass, having the harps of God. And they sing the song of Moses the servant of God, and the song of the Lamb, saying, Great and marvellous are thy works, Lord God Almighty; just and true are thy ways, thou King of saints."

God's people in the end get the victory over the beast power. They get the victory over self-worship. They get the victory over the idea that they can challenge their Creator or change His times and laws. They get the victory over pride and selfishness. They get the victory over independence. They stand on the sea of glass and sing this song.

God says about these people that they are faultless—not only blameless, but faultless. It reminds us of Romans 8:29: "For whom he did foreknow, he also did predestinate to be conformed to the image of his Son." I would certainly like to look more at the image of Jesus than at the image to the beast, wouldn't you? I would want to conform to the image of God's Son rather than conform to the image of the beast. There will be heavy issues at the end of time. Daniel and Revelation indicate clearly that people are going to face death over a day of worship. We wonder how it could happen, but that's the prediction.

At that time you can belong to one of two groups. One group cannot buy or sell and faces death. But Jesus says,

"Your bread and water will be sure." See Isaiah 33:16. David wrote, Psalm 37:25: "I have been young, and now am old; yet have I not seen the righteous forsaken, nor his seed begging bread." Revelation 2:10: "Be thou faithful unto death, and I will give thee a crown of life."

On the other hand are the seven last plagues with no place to hide and no hope for a future beyond the grave.

That's why I like the childhood memory of sitting around the fire on Friday evening and reciting Psalm 91. It may have become routine then, but it will not be routine when we face the closing scenes of history. Let's read that psalm together: "He that dwelleth in the secret place of the most High shall abide under the shadow of the Almighty. I will say of the Lord, He is my refuge and my fortress: my God; in him will I trust. Surely he shall deliver thee from the snare of the fowler, and from the noisome pestilence. He shall cover thee with his feathers, and under his wings shalt thou trust: his truth shall be thy shield and buckler. Thou shalt not be afraid for the terror by night; nor for the arrow that flieth by day; nor for the pestilence that walketh in darkness; nor for the destruction that wasteth at noonday. A thousand shall fall at thy side, and ten thousand at thy right hand; but it shall not come nigh thee. Only with thine eyes shalt thou behold and see the reward of the wicked. Because thou hast made the Lord, which is my refuge, even the most High, thy habitation; there shall no evil befall thee, neither shall any plague come nigh thy dwelling. For he shall give his angels charge over thee, to keep thee in all thy ways. They shall bear thee up in their hands, lest thou dash thy foot against a stone. Thou shalt tread upon the lion and adder: the young lion and the dragon shalt thou trample under feet. Because he hath set his love upon me, therefore will I deliver him: I will set him on high, because he hath known my name. He shall call upon me, and I will answer him: I will be with him in trouble; I will deliver him, and honour him. With long life will I satisfy him, and shew him my salvation."

You can't miss if you're on God's side. You may die, although there's a better word for it—you may *sleep*. Huss and Jerome went to sleep. John the Baptist went to sleep. The apostle Paul went to sleep. Sleep is not all bad. And the long life with which God has promised to satisfy His people will last throughout eternity.

Would you like to have the seal and name of God written on your forehead? God offers this marvelous privilege to you as you come to Him, and continue coming to Him as long as time lasts. Nobody writes his name on something unless it belongs to him. When God's name is written on our foreheads, it will be because we belong to Him and will be His forever.

Real Christians Never Die

Have you ever attended a good funeral? That doesn't even sound right does it? The words *good* and *funeral* don't seem to have any logical relationship. But I have come away from funerals saying, "That was a good funeral." I hope you will keep reading long enough to understand what I mean

We have been studying the pillars of the Adventist faith. This last one is sometimes referred to as "the state of the dead." Whoever came up with that phrase, I don't know. We are studying in these last two chapters the condition of man in death and what the Bible says about it.

Let's begin by reading John 11, verses 1 to 4 and 11 to 14: "Now a certain man was sick, named Lazarus, of Bethany, the town of Mary and her sister Martha." Verse 3: "Therefore his sisters sent unto him, saying, Lord, behold, he whom thou lovest is sick. When Jesus heard that, he said, This sickness is not unto death." Notice that last phrase, "This sickness is not unto death." You know as well as I do that Lazarus died, or at least that's what we call what happened to him. Jesus, apparently indifferent, remained where He was for two days, so that He did not arrive in Bethany until four days later. Verse 6: "He abode two days in the same place where he was." Then verse 11: "After that he saith unto them, Our friend Lazarus sleepeth; but I

109

go, that I may awake him out of sleep. Then said his disciples, Lord, if he sleep, he shall do well. Howbeit Jesus spake of his death: but they thought that he had spoken of taking of rest in sleep. Then said Jesus unto them plainly, Lazarus is dead." Notice that Jesus used the word *death* reluctantly. He preferred to say *sleep*.

Seventh-day Adventists are among the few people in the Christian religious world who believe, concerning the condition of man in death, that he is unconscious in the grave until the morning of the resurrection when Jesus comes again. We are definitely in the minority in this belief. Most of Christendom today believes that people go to their reward in some way at the time of what we call death.

But we believe in the importance of this doctrine as it is taught in Scripture. It is one of the major areas which the enemy concentrated on when he launched the sin problem in this world. If you go back to the Garden of Eden, you discover the first spiritualistic seance. Using the medium of a serpent, the devil presented three falsehoods. First, you don't have to do what God says. Second, if you disobey God, the penalty won't be what He says it will be; you won't die. Third, "Ye shall be as gods, knowing good and evil." You don't need a dependent relationship upon God. You're good enough. Leave fellowship with God for drunkards and harlots and thieves. These three points worked so well for the devil in the Garden of Eden that he has hung onto them like a bulldog ever since. They are the three major deceptions he will use just before the end.

In the subject of the condition of mankind in death, we find a beautiful sample of how to let the Bible interpret itself. For example, we all know about Luke 23:43 and Jesus' words to the thief on the cross: "Verily I say unto thee, To day shalt thou be with me in paradise." Millions of people have used this verse to prove that when a man dies he goes directly to Paradise. But you should never base your belief on a single verse. The Protestant approach to Scriptural interpretation is to look up everything you can find from Bible writers on a given topic; then find out what the balance of information is.

So we find other verses that describe the condition of mankind in death. Psalm 146:4 says, "His breath goeth forth, he returneth to his earth; in that very day his thoughts perish." Ecclesiastes 9:5, 6 adds, "The living know that they shall die: but the dead know not any thing, neither have they any more a reward; for the memory of them is forgotten. Also their love, and their hatred, and their envy, is now perished; neither have they any more a portion for ever in any thing that is done under the sun." As you continue to examine the weight of evidence, you can only conclude that man is unconscious in his grave until Jesus comes again.

But you still have Luke 23:43 to deal with. You may wonder how to get it together with the rest of the Bible's teaching on the subject. So you go back. You check the context, and you find that the thief did not go to Paradise that day, because he didn't even die that day. Read John 19:31-33. You also find that Jesus Himself did not go to Paradise that day, because He said so three days later. Read John 20:17. Then you discover that a comma is misplaced in Luke 23:43. At last the text begins to come clear. Instead of saying, "I say unto thee, Today . . . ," it should read, "I say unto you today, . . . "

As significant as this is, perhaps the most exciting part of this topic is what Jesus had to say concerning death as recorded in the story of Lazarus.

In the days of Jesus, death was a dread mystery. Even the religious leaders were at each other's throats on the subject. In those days you could hear Pharisees and Sadducees arguing loud and long on street corners concerning whether or not there was life after death. The Pharisees believed there *was* life after death, the Sadducees did not—that's why they were Sad-you-see! No real hope in the future. No joy!

You may recall that the apostle Paul stood one day before a counsel of these people. The heat was on Paul. He cleverly took the heat away from himself by bringing up the question of the resurrection. Immediately, the Pharisees and Sadducees were at each other's throats. Paul may have stood there smiling as the pressure on himself abated.

In the midst of this kind of confusion and complexity, Jesus came and said, "I am the resurrection and the life. He that believeth in me, though he were dead, yet shall he live." He gave us a word of certainty on the subject of death and the resurrection. All through the Gospel of John we find Jesus' teaching on the subject. John 6:50: "This is the bread which cometh down from heaven, that a man may eat thereof, and not die." Verse 51: "I am the living bread which came down from heaven: if any man eat of this bread, he shall live forever." Verse 58: "This is that bread which came down from heaven: . . . he that eateth of this bread shall live for ever." And in John 11:26, in our chapter on the story of Lazarus, Jesus said, "Whosoever liveth and believeth in me shall never die."

When a person accepts Jesus, eternal life begins, and he will never die. I recognize that for an Adventist minister to take the position that Christians do not die is a new departure. But I take that position, and I feel in good company, because I believe it is what Jesus taught. "Whosoever liveth and believeth in me shall never die."

Sometimes in our attempts to make sure that people understand clearly the Bible premise that man is in an unconscious state in death, we have gone overboard and tried too hard to make sure that the dead are really dead! In the process, we may have taken away some of the hope and comfort and peace that Jesus offers those who are facing what we call death.

What did Jesus call death? He called it sleep. Not only in

the case of Lazarus, but also in Mark 5. Referring to the little girl, He said, "She's not dead, she's only sleeping." They laughed Him to scorn. But what we call death, He calls sleep.

In encouraging us to think of death as sleep, Jesus taught some very important facts about the condition of mankind in death. What do we think of when we speak of sleep? Is sleep a conscious or an unconscious state? It's unconscious, isn't it?

I remember my father in evangelistic meetings trying to reason with the people on the sawdust trail concerning this question. He said, "If you were to hit a person on the head with a crowbar just hard enough to knock him out, we would say he was unconscious. But if you were to hit him a little harder, so that you killed him, then according to popular belief, he would be conscious again! It doesn't even make sense on the basis of logic and reason. If the popular beliefs were true, then you probably would have done him a favor by hitting him hard enough to kill him—and you could congratulate yourself on that favor while you sat it out in jail."

Even without examining all the Bible evidence on the subject, Jesus' analogy of sleep suggests the unconscious state.

There is something else suggested by the use of the word *sleep*. Sleeping is not all bad, because after sleep comes the waking up time. When you go to sleep looking forward to morning, sleep is not all bad. When you sleep, you are unaware of the passing of time. Abel went to sleep over 5000 years ago, but when he wakes up again, it will seem to have been but a moment. The last saint who falls asleep before Jesus returns will have been in his grave just as long, so far as he is concerned, as was Abel. For both of them it will be but a brief time.

Sleep is not all bad when you consider the reality that all

who believe in Jesus will wake up at the same time, to share and enjoy together the fantastic joy of Jesus' coming again. Have you ever planned together, as a family perhaps, for some surprise? And have you ever said, "Don't begin until we're all there"?

Sleeping is not all bad when you remember the key phrases in this Bible account of the raising of Lazarus. "This sickness is not unto death." "I go that I may awake him out of sleep."

Have you ever considered why there are funerals? Some people today consider funerals to be pagan. Some pull away from funerals altogether; they say to the director, "Cremate him and scatter the ashes from an airplane." There are many methods and gimmicks nowadays.

As a beginning minister, I had problems figuring out a reason for the funeral service. I questioned why we should prolong it one moment longer. Why wait a few days and then gather together with friends and loved ones? There would have to be a Bible reason—and I found it! It's in Ecclesiastes 7:2-4: "It is better to go to the house of mourning, than to go to the house of feasting." Why, Solomon! We thought you were wise! What are you talking about? How can you say that it's better to go to a funeral than to a banquet? Then he gives his reason. "It is better to go to the house of mourning, than to go to the house of feasting: for that is the end of all men; and the living will lay it to his heart. Sorrow is better than laughter: for by the sadness of the countenance the heart is made better. The heart of the wise is in the house of mourning; but the heart of fools is in the house of mirth."

What is he saying? When you go into the presence of what we call death, you are forced to consider the issues of time and eternity. The clock stands still. You are sitting, as it were, in the very presence of God. People who have been used to not thinking can't help but think. Their only other option is to stay away or get drunk. And, of course, that is what a lot of people do. They have to have a few drinks under their belt!

But I believe God's presence is very close on several major occasions in His church. If you have had your eyes open, you have discovered His presence in a special way at the communion service. Another time when He is especially close is at a baptism; you can almost sense the angels of God rejoicing at such a time. I also believe that the presence of God is close at a funeral service. That's what I mean by a good funeral.

"The heart of the wise is in the house of mourning; but the heart of fools is in the house of mirth." Wise people go to funerals; fools go only to parties. How much thinking do you do about time and eternity at a banquet? How much thinking do you do about time and eternity at a funeral?

Sometimes we have missed the purpose of the Christian funeral. We become obsessed with proving what a great person the deceased was. We deliver eulogy after eulogy, and the name of Jesus Christ is hardly mentioned. It's like standing in front of the king of some great country and saying, "But I was sergeant-at-arms of my freshman class!"

It is not the dead person who counts at a funeral service; it is the living God who counts. Although man is worth everything in the eyes of the universe, his greatest achievements are as nothing in the presence of the great God of heaven. People who will someday stand upon the sea of glass will say, "Great and marvellous are thy works, Lord God Almighty; just and true are thy ways, thou King of saints." Revelation 15:3. People who know God today will be saying the same thing at funerals.

I've had people ask, "How could you conduct that funeral? Wasn't it a hard one?" Perhaps there had been a suicide, or the deceased was known to be openly against God. I don't talk about people at funerals; I talk about Jesus. The greatest testimony in anyone's behalf is that Jesus loved him, more than anyone else ever did and has done everything possible to see him in His kingdom.

A funeral is not for the purpose of deciding anyone's destiny. How often we gather together and say, "This was a good person." He may have been the town scoundrel, but at his funeral we give him good marks. We say, "Oh, but he had a good heart. He did something nice for Widow Brown years ago. He paid his taxes once." We try as hard as we can to assure ourselves that our loved one will make it into the kingdom.

In fact, if you were to go by the relatives and friends, it's seldom if ever you hear of anyone not making it! But this is not our business—it has never been our business. We can only look on the outward appearance; it is God who looks on the heart. We would be far better off to keep silent on this subject. We all know that the day will come when people we thought sure were going to be in God's kingdom will be missing, and others we thought sure would be missing will be there. We are going to be surprised. So it would be far better for us to be silent now.

As we gather together in times of sorrow, if we could see as God sees, what a difference it would make. The hardest trial, the greatest tragedy, the heaviest heart would be comforted if we could only see that what we call time is but a drop in the bucket. And time, whether it's 6 years or 60 years or 960 years, will seem as nothing in comparison to eternity.

There are blessings in sleep. Here's a comment concerning Adam, from *Patriarchs and Prophets,* page 82: "Adam's life was one of sorrow, humility, and contrition. When he left Eden, the thought that he must die thrilled him with horror. . . . Though the sentence of death pronounced upon him by his Maker had at first appeared terrible, yet after beholding for nearly a thousand years the results of sin, he felt that it was merciful in God to bring to an end a life of suffering and sorrow." Adam was glad to lie down and go to sleep. Could it be possible that God knows that the most we can take of this life is three score years and ten, and that, if by reason of strength we live four score years, yet those extra years are "labor and sorrow"? See Psalm 90:10.

When we realize that what we call death is no problem to God, it takes away some of the sting. Death is no problem to God. It never has been. When Jesus wept at the tomb of Lazarus, He was not weeping because of the problem of death. He was the Life-giver. No, He wept because of unbelief. Jesus can deal with death far easier than He can with unbelief.

One day a friend of mine and I were in a cemetery after a service. The crowds had gone away, but we stayed. This one had come close. We watched as the cemetery workers lowered the heavy concrete lid and began to pour the cement. I said to my friend, "Do you suppose the angels will be able to get through all that cement?" I wasn't trying to be funny, only to make a point.

He looked at me, startled, and then he understood. He smiled and replied, "That will be no problem. Don't you worry about that."

No, I'm not worried about that. To the believer, death is but a small matter. God has prepared to more than make up to us for all of the unfairness of being born here. When Jesus comes again, He will have no problem waking up His sleeping children.

Down in Texas some years ago, a little six-year-old girl was stricken ill. Doctors looked serious right from the beginning. Then she went to sleep. The day of the funeral came. Friends and loved ones gathered. As the father, who was an unbeliever, came by the casket, he said with bitterness, "Good-bye. Good-bye forever."

Then the mother came by. She was a godly woman who

believed in Jesus and what Jesus had to say about death. She leaned over and kissed the little girl and said, "Good night, sweetheart. We've had six wonderful years together. Good night. Mamma will see you in the morning, at the daybreak, when the shadows flee away."

What makes the difference? Jesus makes the difference. I can picture Jesus in the glory land walking in front of the empty mansions. One day He sees that the time clock has run out. As He looks down, He sees not only Lazarus, but thousands sleeping, a great multitude that no man can number. He says to His angels, "My friends are sleeping. But I go that I may awake them out of sleep. It's time for them to come and enjoy living in these mansions we have prepared for them."

What a day! What a hope! "Amid the reeling of the earth, the flash of lightning, and the roar of thunder, the voice of the Son of God calls forth the sleeping saints. He looks upon the graves of the righteous, then, raising His hands to heaven, He cries, 'Awake, Awake, Awake, ye that sleep in the dust, and arise!' Throughout the length and breadth of the earth the dead shall hear that voice, and they that hear shall live. . . . From the prison house of death they come, clothed with immortal glory. . . . The living righteous and the risen saints unite their voices in a long, glad shout of victory." "Little children are borne by holy angels to their mothers' arms. Friends long separated by death are united, nevermore to part, and with songs of gladness ascend together to the city of God."—*The Great Controversy,* pages 644, 645.

The Life in Christ

A long list of unpleasant words begin with the letter *d*. There are *darkness* and *defeat* and *dismay* and *despair* and *doubt* and *discouragement* and *disaster, distress, discord,* and *discontent*. The most dreaded of all, however, and the theme of many a dismal dirge, is the word *death!* Thank God for the other side of the picture presented in His Word! "This is the record, that God hath given to us eternal life, and this life is in his Son." 1 John 5:11.

I'd like to direct your attention first of all to 1 Corinthians 15:3, 4. Ordinarily we don't consider this a reference to the condition of man in death, but there's a double meaning to this passage that I'd like to share with you. "I delivered unto you first of all that which I also received, how that Christ died for our sins according to the scriptures; and that he was buried, and that he rose again the third day according to the scriptures." If we are familiar with life at all, we are very much aware that we are going to die, according to the Scriptures; and that we are going to be buried, undoubtedly. But we can also be very much aware, if we are familiar with Scripture, that we can rise again, according to the Scriptures. We can be thankful for that!

Well, when Seventh-day Adventists were in their beginning stages, back there in the middle of the last century, they had a real struggle with this doctrine. It took them close to ten years to accept it, to the middle of the 1850s. Until that time, they were in line with the main evangelical bodies who believed in the immortality of the soul.

The pioneers actually resisted any other thought. But they found that their belief concerning the immortality of the soul was coming into collision with the other doctrines they had hammered out through sincere Bible study and prayer. For instance, they had discovered the pre-advent judgment in which the cases of all who had ever been among God's people were reviewed before Jesus' return. They pictured some of the early inhabitants of our world, such as the first one who committed murder, the son of Adam and Eve. If you believe in the immortality of the soul, you believe that Cain has been suffering in the flames of eternally burning hell for many years. Then comes the judgment. Cain says, "I beg your pardon? After I've been here in these flames nearly 6000 years, now you want to judge me? No, thanks. You can keep your judgment."

Well, that might be getting a little too literal, but the incongruity of believing in the pre-advent judgment as well as the immortality of the soul was quite apparent. The two doctrines didn't add up.

The pioneers struggled with the realization that spiritualism was gaining a stronghold. The Fox sisters had already given publicity to spiritualistic encounters. Spiritualism is based on the premise that if some part of man does not die but continues to exist somewhere, we should be able to get in touch with it. The early Adventist believers found some of the hard things the Bible has to say about spiritualism, and warnings against it, and this didn't add up.

Then the pioneers came face to face with the big question of how a God of love can allow people to suffer forever in eternal flames. Many people have become atheists because of that teaching, for if a soul is immortal and does not go to heaven, it has to go somewhere else. As Clarence Darrow, the famous lawyer who debated with Bryan, said, "If God sends people to burn forever in hell because they don't accept Him, then that would not be a god, that would be a devil." He said, "This is precisely why I am an agnostic."

It's very interesting that a large number of preachers who have been polled in recent years no longer believe in the doctrine of eternally burning hellfire, because it doesn't make sense to them either.

It certainly did not make sense to the Missouri newspaper editor who wrote the following: "If an endless hell of torment for the wicked is a necessary part of God's plan, and if God has to have a devil employed to run the place and keep the fire going, then there is simply no getting around the fact that God and the devil are business associates and good friends. If there is an endless hell of torment in God's scheme at all, it is a very important part of the scheme. And surely God would not appoint His very worst enemy to such an important position as general superintendent of hell.

"Suppose, for the sake of argument, that God needs an endless hell in His business, and suppose that God had employed His enemy to run the place. Do you not see that the enemy could take advantage of God and let the fire go smack out, or that he might go to the other extreme and waste the brimstone or burn out the flues and do much damage that way? Where there was so much fire, there would be constant danger of having the whole place burn up; so you see God would need a man on the job that He could trust, one who could be depended upon to run hell in a perfectly honest and Christianlike manner.

"Now, brother, I put it to you plainly and honestly: If the devil is as mean and low-down and tricky as people say he is, do you honestly believe God would keep such a character on His payroll throughout eternity and trust him with the all-important business affairs of the everlasting fireworks? What do you think about it?"

So the early Advent believers found that a number of teachings of the church came into collision with the belief of the immortality of the soul.

Some began pressing heavily for a rethinking of this position concerning the condition of mankind in death. But others of the early pioneer leaders said that it would bring ill repute upon the little group if they broke away from the main body and took the position that death is a sleep. They advocated caution. This was the reason for the struggle and the johnny-come-lately acceptance of this pillar of our faith.

In the end, however, they made use of the Protestant approach to Scripture and searched out all they could find on the topic, rather than taking a passage of Scripture here and there. They came to their conclusions based on the weight of evidence.

Let's follow this approach now as we seek to understand what the Bible says on the subject. We'll ask a few questions with a regular old Bible catechism approach.

WHERE ARE THE DEAD?

1. How and when do we receive eternal life? "This is the will of him that sent me, that every one which seeth the Son and *believeth on him,* may have everlasting life: and I will raise him up *at the last day.*" John 6:40.

2. What about death and sorrow until the "last day"? "I would not have you to be ignorant, brethren, concerning them which are *asleep,* that ye sorrow not, even as others which have no hope." 1 Thessalonians 4:13.

3. What is that hope? "The Lord himself shall descend from heaven with a shout, with the voice of the archangel, and with the trump of God: and the dead in Christ shall rise." 1 Thessalonians 4:16.

4. Where are the dead when they hear the Lord's voice? "Marvel not at this: for the hour is coming, in the which all that are *in their graves* shall hear his voice, and shall come forth." John 5:28.

5. Is everlasting life given to those who don't believe? "He that believeth on the Son hath everlasting life: and he that believeth not the Son shall not see life." "For God so loved the world, that he gave his only begotten Son, that whosoever believeth in him should not perish, but have everlasting life." John 3:36, 16.

NOTE: There are only two choices—they are opposites—to perish or have everlasting life.

6. Does man go to his reward at death or at Jesus' coming? "The Son of man shall come in the glory of his Father with his angels; and *then* he shall reward every man according to his works." Matthew 16:27.

7. What then should be our determination? "I pray God your whole *spirit* and *soul* and *body* be preserved blameless unto the coming of our Lord Jesus Christ." 1 Thessalonians 5:23.

THE NATURE OF MAN UNTIL JESUS COMES

8. What happens to the spirit, soul and body of those who "fall asleep" now? "Then shall the dust [or body] return to the earth as it was: and the spirit shall return unto God who gave it." Ecclesiastes 12:7.

9. What is this "spirit"? "All the while my breath is in me, and the spirit of God [the breath which God gave him] is in my nostrils." Job 27:3.

10. What then is taken away, or returns to God at death? "Thou

takest away their *breath*, they die, and return to their dust."
Psalm 104:29.

11. What is the soul? "The Lord God formed man of the dust
of the ground, and breathed into his nostrils the breath of
life; and man *became* a living soul." Genesis 2:7.

NOTE: The formula for a living soul is therefore the following: Dust + breath of life = living soul. Death is the "oppo-
site of life" (Webster). Therefore the formula for death is
this: living soul − breath of life = dust.

12. Does the soul really die? "The soul that sinneth, it shall
die." Ezekiel 18:20.

NOTE: The *combination* of electricity and a light bulb produces light. Take away either the current or the bulb and the
light is gone. Where did it go? It didn't go anywhere! It simply no longer exists! So it is with the soul. At death it no
longer exists because the two ingredients that make the soul
are separated.

MAN—CONSCIOUS OR UNCONSCIOUS IN DEATH?

13. Is there anything conscious about man in death? "His breath
goeth forth, he returneth to his earth; in that very day his
thoughts perish." Psalm 146:4.

NOTE: The *breath* goes back to God. But the breath cannot
think.

14. Can we communicate with the dead or the dead with us? "The
living know that they shall die: but the *dead know not any
thing.*" "Their love, and their hatred, and their envy, is
now perished." "There is no work, nor device, nor knowledge, nor wisdom, in the grave, whither thou goest." Ecclesiastes 9:5, 6, 10.

NOTE: The dead have no thoughts or feelings to communicate!

15. Where did we get the idea that man does not die? *"The serpent* said unto the woman, Ye shall not surely die." Genesis 3:4.

NOTE: This was *the devil's* lie. If the devil's lie were the truth, God must have lied when He said, "Thou shalt surely die." Genesis 2:17. Did Adam and Eve's transgression bring sin, sickness, and death, or did it bring life? If the devil told the truth, there is no death. If there is no death, why did Jesus have to "come that they might have *life"?* John 10:10. Certainly it is unthinkable that God should sacrifice His Son to keep a race of people who *couldn't* die, from dying?

Let's change the picture now and look at the spiritual truth found in death and resurrection.

Romans 6:3, 4: "Know ye not, that so many of us as were baptized into Jesus Christ were baptized into his death? Therefore we are buried with him by baptism into death." That's justification, dying to our past sins. Verse 4: "Therefore we are buried with him by baptism into death: that like as Christ was raised up from the dead by the glory of the Father, even so we also should walk in newness of life." That's sanctification, dying to our present sinning.

This truth shows up repeatedly; for instance, 2 Corinthians 5:14 also speaks of justification. Look these texts up for yourself. Also Galatians 2:20: "I am crucified with Christ."

When we come to sanctification, there is a list of texts that remind us of the comparison between living the Christian life and resurrection. Romans 6:4-7; 2 Corinthians 5:15; 1 Peter 2:24; Colossians 3:1-4; Romans 8:1-10; and Ephesians 2:1-10 all use the resurrection as a symbol of sanctification, rising to walk in newness of life.

Revelation 14, the chapter we have been studying, contains an interesting verse. We have often understood it one way, but it can also be understood another way. Verse 13: "I heard a voice from heaven saying unto me, Write, Blessed are the dead which die in the Lord from henceforth: Yea, saith the Spirit, that they may rest from their labours; and their works do follow them."

We are familiar with the idea of tombstones and cemeteries and pioneers. But please look at the spiritual impact of this verse in the light of the resurrection and the idea of walking in newness of life. "Blessed are the dead which die in the Lord." Jesus spoke of taking up our cross daily. Paul also used the cross as a symbol of dying to self. And as we have a relationship with Jesus, one to one, day by day, we discover what it means to go to the cross with Jesus and be buried with Him. "Blessed are the dead which die in the Lord" in this sense as well.

"That they may rest from their labours." As we have noticed, the key word in the Sabbath commandment is *rest*. Hebrews 4 speaks of resting from our work of trying to sanctify ourselves or justify ourselves or work our way to heaven. Jesus' invitation is to come, all who labor and are heavy-laden, and He will give us rest. Here you have the dead who die in the Lord, who rest from their labors, "and their works do follow them." What a verse to dwell on as we think of the truth of sanctification by faith, of knowing what it means not only to accept God's forgiveness, but to accept life through Christ today and tomorrow and next week, until He comes again.

It is one thing to say, "I believe," and quite another to *really* believe. Life eternal comes not to those who know *about* Jesus but to those who *know* Jesus. See John 17:3. This personal acquaintance with the Lord Jesus Christ comes to every believer through the study of His Word and through prayer. Our personal acquaintance with Jesus is just as strong or as weak as is our daily experience in these two avenues. As we prayerfully open the Bible and contemplate the greatest story ever told, we discover that "Christ was treated as we deserve, that we might be treated as He deserves. He was condemned for our sins, in which He had no share, that we might be saved by His righteousness, in which we had no share. He suffered the death which was ours, that we might receive the life which was his."—*The Desire of Ages,* p. 25.

This is what breaks the sinner's heart and brings the mind into captivity to the will of God! Herein lies our hope of eternal life.

The golden morning is fast approaching;
Jesus soon will come
To take His faithful and happy children
To their promised home.

O, we see the gleams of the golden morning
Piercing through this night of gloom!
O, we see the gleams of the golden morning
That will burst the tomb.

SUMMARY

As you have come to understand the basis for these six major pillars of the Seventh-day Adventist faith, you have been introduced to the very heart of Adventism in terms of the beliefs that are distinct from those of the majority of the Christian world today.

These beliefs are not, as many have supposed, some legalistic maneuver to try to earn salvation by our own works. They provide instead a beautiful illustration of the plan of salvation. The two great truths of Christ's sacrifice for us at the cross and of the work that He wants to do in living His life in us are found interwoven throughout.

The three angels of Revelation bear primarily a message *for* the everlasting gospel of Jesus Christ, not *against* the beast. The pre-advent judgment highlights God's love and mercy in making clear to all the reasons for His decisions in the judgment. The law of God reveals His character and His power to reveal Himself through His children. The faith of Jesus is offered to make His life our own. The Sabbath rest shows how we may rest from our own works, through accepting of His rest. And the condition of mankind in death reminds us of the continuing invitation of Jesus to die to self and rise to walk in newness of life with Him.

It is our hope that the study of this *Uncommon Ground* has led you closer to Him, whom to know is life eternal.